THE ULTIMATE JOB HUNTER'S GUIDEBOOK

FOURTH EDITION

THE ULTIMATE JOB HUNTER'S GUIDEBOOK

Susan D. Greene
Greene Marketing & Advertising

Melanie C. L. Martel
New Hampshire Technical Institute

Houghton Mifflin Company
Boston   New York

V.P., Editor-in-Chief: George T. Hoffman
Technology Manager/Development Editor: Damaris C. Curran
Assistant Editor: Julia M. Perez
Associate Project Editor: Kristin Penta
Editorial Assistant: Lisa C. Sullivan
Senior Production/Design Coordinator: Jodi O'Rourke
Senior Manufacturing Coordinator: Marie Barnes
Senior Marketing Manager: Steven W. Mikels
Marketing Associate: Lisa E. Boden

Cover illustration by Jim Dryden.

To the best of our knowledge, the information published in *The Ultimate Job Hunter's Guidebook* is correct and accurate at the time of publication. However, the text is intended only as a guide. Use your best judgment as related to your individual situation when applying the recommendations in this book.

Chapter opener illustrations by Neverne Covington.

Illustration on page 4 by Mark Penta.

Printed in the U.S.A.

Library of Congress Control Number: 2002109468

ISBN: 0-618-30298-0

23456789–MV–07 06 05 04

CONTENTS IN BRIEF

CONTENTS

PREFACE

Job hunting. Just the thought of it gives most of us an uneasy feeling. Where do you look? Whom should you call? What if you can't find anything in your field? Whether you're about to graduate, an experienced professional, or someone returning after a leave of absence from the job market, simply getting started can be a tremendous hurdle.

This book is designed to help you move past that incapacitating inertia and get your career on track. Written in conversational language, this fourth edition of *The Ultimate Job Hunter's Guidebook* takes you through the steps necessary to define your goals, create a winning résumé, write effective cover letters, generate job leads, and interview with confidence.

Organization of This Book

The Ultimate Job Hunter's Guidebook features four parts: Setting Your Course, Gathering Your Tools, Beginning the Search, and Getting to Work. Each part speaks to a different phase of the job-hunting process. Short on theory but long on straightforward, easy-to-follow advice, the book gives practical tips intended to help you excel in your immediate job search as well as your career over the long term.

Much of *The Ultimate Job Hunter's Guidebook, Fourth Edition* is dedicated to the all-encompassing question of how to find potential employers. We review the typical methods, and we propose many nontraditional strategies. The book also includes detailed instruction on how to take advantage of the new technologies revolutionizing today's job market. You'll discover the resources available on the Internet, such as databases that provide employers with instant access to your résumé, online classified ads from around the country, and company profiles that make research about employers easy.

Finally, we offer numerous success stories of people who've made it. Their career sagas are inspirational, motivational, and most importantly, educational. From their stories, you'll learn that no matter how challenging your job hunt may seem at first, with a little hard work and creativity you can accomplish your goals.

New Features

In addition to updating the material in *The Ultimate Job Hunter's Guidebook, Fourth Edition,* we've added some new features. At the beginning of each chapter, you'll find a *Learning Objectives* section that previews the upcoming material and facilitates student focus. We've also included opening vignettes entitled *Strategies in Action,* to demonstrate real-life application of the material contained in the chapter.

In the résumé chapter (Chapter 6), in addition to information and résumé samples for recent graduates and first-time job hunters, you'll now find material relevant to individuals who have significant work experience and are applying for high-level professional positions.

New and revised exercises throughout the text, as well as reorganization of the book's material, make this fourth edition an extremely user-friendly learning tool.

Web Site

Because we believe that one of the keys to a successful job hunt is to gather as much information as possible, we've created a comprehensive web site as a companion tool for *The Ultimate Job Hunter's Guidebook, Fourth Edition.* The web site expands on many of the subjects covered in the text to enhance both teaching and student learning. To aid in classroom lectures, downloadable PowerPoint slides and discussion questions are available on the Instructor Web Site.

The Student Web Site offers chapter summaries and ACE self-tests to enhance understanding of the *Guidebook*'s material, many supplemental articles by renowned career experts, and direct links to many other useful career web sites. You can visit the companion web site for the text at **http://college.hmco.com.**

Acknowledgments

We would like to thank the following people, who have reviewed this text and the previous editions, for their many valuable comments:

Susan Borovsky, *DeVry Institute of Technology*
Nicol Burnett, *Harding Business College*
Elaine DePasquale, *Robert Morris College*
Wendy Edson, *Hilbert College*
Tedd Farrar, *Virginia College*
Robert Greenberg, *University of Tennessee*
Melody Hunt, *Indiana Business College*
Donna Jarrett, *Bradford School*
Cheryl Kaufman, *Goshen College*
Donna Lazzell, *Westwood College of Technology*
John McCarty, *Mansfield Business College*
Johanna McDowell, *ITT Technical Institute*
April McDuffie, *East Central Technical College*
E. Kathleen Pollack, *Bryant and Statton College*
Teresa Quesenberry, *Blue Mountain Community College*
Rebecca Simoneaux, *Blair Junior College*
Dwight Wilson, *Indiana Business College*

We Want to Hear from You

Please keep the following questions in mind as you use this text during your job hunt. How is your job hunt progressing? Which ideas and suggestions in the fourth edition of *The Ultimate Job Hunter's Guidebook* have been most helpful? Which subjects would you have liked to learn more about? What was enlightening? Motivating? Mystifying? Write down your comments, suggestions, and job-hunting success stories, and send them to us.

Houghton Mifflin Company
College Business
222 Berkeley Street
Boston, MA 02116
college_bus@hmco.com

We'll gladly read your feedback and use it to make the next edition of *The Ultimate Job Hunter's Guidebook* an even better career tool. Thank you!

Susan D. Greene
Melanie C. L. Martel

THE ULTIMATE JOB HUNTER'S GUIDEBOOK

Part One

SETTING YOUR COURSE

Planning Your Job Search

Learning Objectives

In this chapter, you will learn to do the following:

- Identify the steps involved in the job-hunting process
- Begin creating a strategic plan for successful employment

Chapter 1

STRATEGIES in ACTION

Ryan anxiously anticipated the next few weeks. Graduation was just around the corner, but lurking in his subconscious there was something he dreaded even more than his upcoming finals—unemployment. Would he be able to find a position in his field? How would he find out about job openings? How should he write his résumé? What should he say in his cover letters? What should he wear to interviews? Just thinking about it all gave him butterflies.

But then Ryan remembered a piece of advice he'd received from one of his favorite professors: When a big task seems overwhelming, break it into smaller, more manageable pieces. And that's what he decided to do with job hunting—identify each of the steps in the process and work toward completing each one successfully. Eventually, he knew, all those little accomplishments would add up and lead him to his final goal—obtaining a good job. Suddenly, the prospect of job hunting didn't seem so scary after all.

Part One: Setting Your Course

The first steps of the job hunt involve choosing a direction, setting goals, and deciding on a strategy for reaching those goals. Although some new job hunters may be anxious to get started on the actual search, some careful planning at the outset will ensure better results.

Conduct a Self-Assessment (see page 10)

The first step in job hunting is to find out about yourself and your desires. Decide what you'd really like to do. What are your skills and capabilities? A little soul-searching at the start of your job hunt can pay big dividends. After you've learned about yourself, you'll be better able to determine what type of employment you'd like to seek.

Research various occupational fields to find a career that matches your skills and desires. Visit your local library and your local college's career-planning and placement offices. Job-shadow people whose careers are potential options for you. If after doing this research you are still unsure, expand your base of information. Work on a self-evaluation with a career counselor, if necessary. Then try to gather more information about the demands of different careers. Choose one or two careers to start with; take some pressure off yourself by remembering that very few people stay in the same career for life. The job you're seeking now is only the first step in a series of career moves.

Job-Search Steps

Next, think about the geographic location where you'd like to live and work. Would you consider relocating? If so, how far? The answers to these questions will determine the literal boundaries of your job search. Consider all the facets of your life that will hinge on the location of your job: housing, commuting, schooling for you and your family, and relationships that will change with distance. After you've thought about these and other pertinent factors, map out your target job-search area. Be prepared to rethink your career focus or target area if you consistently hit dead ends.

Target Potential Employers (see page 24)

Who employs people with your skills? Which companies are best, and which positions within them are likely to fit your interests and abilities? There are many places you can look for answers to these questions.

For written material, start at the library. Check out manufacturing and industrial directories. Find the appropriate professional journals and do a periodic search to see what current newspapers and magazines have to say about a particular company or a general career field (a librarian can help you). College placement offices often have information on local companies. The local chamber of commerce or professional and business associations can also provide you with helpful literature. You might also glean valuable information from classified ads and the Yellow Pages. The Internet will surely also be a key component of your investigation. Use it to research industries, find want ads, and learn about individual companies. There are also numerous employment sites on the Web; some time spent "surfing" will give you an idea of the scope of information that is available.

Your most valuable source of information, however, is people. Be persistent and thorough. Let everyone you know help with your job search. Ask questions of friends, relatives, and coworkers. See what you can learn from members of your church, health club, social organizations, or professional groups. Person-to-person contact provides you with current information and the "inside scoop" on companies or careers. Talking with people is a great way to begin establishing your network. You'll learn about various types of jobs and may even eventually get tips about specific job openings. Networking is valuable preparation for interviewing; it is in general an increasingly important skill in the workplace. This is also the point at which you could begin informational interviewing, to benefit from the knowledge of established professionals.

All your reading and networking should pay off in enabling you to create a long list of possible employers. Narrow down this list to those who meet the requirements you set in the first phases of your job search. Set aside organizations that are outside your geographical range or that do not employ people in the type of position you seek.

Now that you have a strong working list, write or call potential employers to request any public relations information, sales literature, or annual reports they are willing to send you. Some or all of that information may even be available at the company's web site. Use these materials or your telephone skills to learn the name of the person who makes the hiring decisions at each workplace. This is usually the person who would be your supervisor. Avoid sending materials to the human resources office; its primary function is to screen out applicants!

Consider All Job Options (see pages 43 and 54)

Remember that part of setting your job-hunting course is to explore *all* options. That may mean giving consideration to some types of employers you didn't include in your original prospect list such as government agencies, nonprofit organizations, or small companies. You may even want to investigate starting your own business. Also consider taking an indirect path to your "dream job" through temping, freelancing, or volunteer work. At this stage of your job search, every idea represents additional opportunities, so get creative!

Part Two: Gathering Your Tools

The next phases of the job hunt involve composing and finding all the documents you need to best present yourself to potential employers. Having a well-prepared résumé and some glowing letters of recommendation, as well as a few samples of your work, will give you a sense of confidence before you begin interviewing.

Prepare Your Résumé (see page 64)

If you were building a home, you'd use the very best tools available to you, to make the process easier and the outcome better. Similarly, when you build your career, it is important to use quality tools. Examine all the résumés you can find. Rely on your best judgment, but also take into account the advice of those who work in your desired field. Make decisions about format, paper, type styles, and wording. Write a few rough drafts and get feedback from trusted friends and professionals. A neat, well-written, and error-free résumé not only gives you confidence throughout your job search, but it can also get you in the door and provide you with the opportunity to sell yourself during a job interview. You may find it beneficial to develop several versions of your résumé, tailored to each of the various jobs you'd consider. Additionally, an Internet version might be necessary if you plan to post your résumé online or send it to employers via e-mail.

Write Cover Letters (see page 108)

Once you have all your tools—your self-assessment, résumé, and research—you can proceed to use them. Write a cover letter (also called a letter of application) to each employer and mail it with your résumé. Your cover letter gives you the chance to state which position you are applying for, mention your strong points, and ask for an interview. You'll probably need to develop several versions and review your drafts with others to double-check the wording and format. Whenever possible, address the cover letter to a specific person. Remember that the best person to send your cover letter to is the person who would be your immediate supervisor, not someone in the human resources department.

Obtain References and Assemble a Portfolio (see page 124)

What supporting documents can you supply that further your assertion that you are a talented individual who is ready and able to work?

The most common documents, letters of reference, can be extremely valuable in convincing an employer to hire you. References serve as third-party endorsements testifying to the quality of your work and character. You can obtain letters of reference from previous employers, teachers, or anyone else you've known professionally. It is never too early to start soliciting letters of recommendation.

A portfolio of your work can also be useful for presentation in an interview. If possible, gather samples of relevant work and your writing, special projects you've completed, awards, or articles written about you or your work that may have been published in your local newspaper.

Part Three: Beginning the Search

At this stage, you have amassed the self-knowledge and the tools to confidently present yourself to employers. You will want to keep track of the many contacts you make and devise a system for following up on each meeting or correspondence. As you interact with those you're considering working with, you'll also need to know what to expect in terms of job applications, interviews, and employment tests to ensure that you make a good impression at every opportunity.

Organize and Survive the Job Hunt (see page 136)

Your job hunt will progress more smoothly if you are organized. Keep notes on the people you've contacted and the next steps in your job search. Make to-do lists and charts so you can have all important data in front of you. File your papers together in a folder so that neither a special document nor an opportunity is lost. Note the time-management and organizational habits of those you consider to be successful.

Take time to assess your progress, and if necessary, try some new job-hunting strategies. Be sure to take care of your physical and emotional well-being. Job hunting can be stressful, and to reach your goals, you must learn to make your stress work for you.

Take Your Job Hunt Online (see page 146)

The Internet is one of the job hunter's best tools. Use it to gather research on careers, trends, industries, and individual companies; search for job openings; post your résumé; exchange correspondence with employers; and network with other job hunters.

Fill Out Job Applications (see page 154)

Some employers may want you to fill out a company application form before they consider you for a job. This small step is your first chance to show the employer the quality of your work. Brush up on the information these forms require so that you'll feel comfortable when the time comes for you to complete one.

Go to Interviews (see page 161)

When you receive that important phone call telling you the date of your interview, begin practicing your interviewing techniques. Prepare a list of personal and professional references to bring with you. Research the company so you can answer the interviewer's questions intelligently. Find the company web site and gather any literature the company publishes. Also prepare your own list of questions about the company and the job.

Arrive for your interview on time and looking your best. Be ready to answer the interviewer's questions with poise and confidence. Watch your body language, voice, and mannerisms.

Consider each interview a learning experience and be prepared to evaluate yourself after each one. Remember that your work is not finished once the interview is over. Think of ways to improve your job-hunting skills, and follow up on the interview with thank-you notes, e-mail messages, and phone calls to remind the employer that you're interested.

Take Employment Tests (see page 196)

Because the costs of hiring and training new employees are so high, employers seek ways to weed out bad candidates. Some of the employment tests you may encounter are drug tests, aptitude tests, psychological tests, and medical exams. A prepared job applicant anticipates this step.

Part Four: Getting to Work

When the preliminary phases of the job search have proved successful, a few long-awaited steps remain. You'll need to evaluate the possibilities you've worked so hard to create and then be sure that your employment gets off to a strong start, all the while keeping an eye on your plans for the future.

Evaluate Job Offers (see page 204)

Your job hunt may be over, but you now face a decision that will have a huge impact on your life. Carefully weigh all your options to make the career choice that is best for you.

Learn Your New Job (see page 214)

The first few months on the job are often fraught with challenges as you meet new people and begin to learn about your specific responsibilities. You may want to adjust your work habits in order to fit in at your workplace. You will need to hone your skills, take in a tremendous amount of information, and familiarize yourself with the corporate culture of your new workplace.

Conducting a
Self-Assessment

In this chapter, you'll take a close look at who you are and what you can offer an employer. You'll use this information to explore various career paths. Specifically, you will:

- Identify your personality, strengths, and skills
- Recognize your assets
- Formulate strategies for personal improvement
- Evaluate your priorities
- Set career goals
- Explore various careers through informational interviews and job shadowing
- Consider taking a career test

Chapter 2

STRATEGIES in ACTION

Henry had spent every summer vacation for the last four years working in his parents' real estate office. He'd helped with marketing, listing, and showing properties, and had interacted with lenders and even sat in on closings. Henry knew he was fortunate to have had so much hands-on experience. Now that he was about to graduate college with a degree in business, however, Henry was facing the biggest decision of his life: Should he return to the family real-estate business, where he knew the ropes and could probably make a decent living as a realtor? Or should he explore other careers that would give him new experiences and opportunities to learn?

Know Yourself

Self-examination is an important step in the job-hunting process. Although at first it may seem a time-consuming distraction from the task of getting your name out to potential employers, it will actually give direction and focus to your search. You'll be better equipped to zero in on the right kind of job. Plus, you'll stand out to employers as someone who really knows what he wants—no wishy-washiness here!

Begin at the Beginning

Perhaps you have always known what career is right for you. Maybe you have been one of the few lucky people who have had insight into their strengths, interests, and values. If so, you have already completed the first step of the job-search process—knowing yourself.

The more common experience for beginning job hunters or those looking to change careers, however, is confusion, nervousness, and lack of direction. The pressure is intense. The task, as many view it, is to choose the perfect career that will provide satisfaction for a lifetime. No wonder some job hunters launch prematurely into fields that are not good choices and do not, as becomes clear later, suit their interests or capabilities. Others spend excessive amounts of time and sweat exploring in an unfocused and unproductive way.

If you begin the pursuit of your next career armed with the knowledge of your strengths, interests, and values, you will improve your motivation and your chances for success. You will also find it easier to set realistic, achievable goals. The next exercise enlists the help of others to help you clarify your self-knowledge. It answers the questions:

- How do others see me?
- What do they see as my strengths?
- How can I apply these strengths to a career?

Valued Perspectives

Before your job search can truly begin, you must be able to identify your personality, strengths, and skills.

Step 1. Interview four people who know you well and whose opinions you value. First, ask each person to list ten words that describe you. (Be sure not to let participants see anyone else's responses.)

Name #1	Name #2	Name #3	Name #4
1.			
2.			
3.			
4.			
5.			
6.			
7.			
8.			
9.			
10.			

Step 2. List the words that tend to be repeated or you feel are especially accurate.

Step 3. Add any words that you think describe you but are not included in the above lists.

Step 4. Rank all the adjectives listed above in order of importance as they relate to career success.

1. _____   6. _____

2. _____   7. _____

3. _____   8. _____

4. _____   9. _____

5. _____   10. _____

Step 5. Examine the common themes and patterns of these responses. Usually, at the very least, those who know you well indicate whether your talents lie in dealing with people, data, or ideas. What seem to be the most common strengths listed by those you surveyed?

_____

Step 6. Brainstorm for connections: How do these strengths translate into job skills? Although answering this question is difficult, it is essential to the usefulness of this exercise.

For example, if your friends and family members have all noted your outgoing personality or unflappable disposition, you might be well-suited for a career that involves working with the public, such as in sales or the service industry. If they've noted you are detail oriented and logical, you might begin exploring a career in computer programming or technical support.

Although you may eventually need the assistance of a professor, a business professional in one of the fields you are considering, or a career counselor, make an initial attempt here to carefully examine the links between your strengths and their workplace applications.

How do these personality traits translate into job skills?

_____

Or, to present the results in another way, list three to five job skills here.

1. _____

2. _____

3. _____

4. _____

5. _____

The results of this exercise may be helpful to refer back to when you are writing a job objective, preparing for an interview, or just feeling unsure of your strengths.

Recognize Your Assets

We all know some things about ourselves that we like and some things that we wish we could change. It's important to focus on your good qualities as you go through life, especially when under the stress associated with job hunting.

EXERCISE

Fill out the following questionnaire and refer to it when you need a boost before an interview.

1. My best personality trait is _____

2. The course in which I did best in school was _____

3. I am good at _____

4. A skill I mastered quickly is _____

5. What I like best about working is _____

6. Good things my teachers or employers have said about me include _____

_____

7. I often receive compliments on _____

_____

8. I have a special talent for _____

_____

9. One obstacle I've overcome is _____

_____

10. I received an award or recognition for _____

_____

11. My most valuable work skill is _____

_____

12. People will enjoy working with me because _____

_____

Reexamine your completions to these sentences. On the following lines, write brief, specific examples of circumstances that illustrate your responses to the questions you've answered above. Focus specifically on the following numbers:

5. _____

7. _____

8. _____

9. _____

11. _____

Take Action to Be Your Best

When you feel good about yourself, others sense your self-confidence. Probably no other quality makes you more marketable as you search for a job. Now is a good time to make some positive moves toward improving how you look and feel, as well as how you perform in the workplace.

EXERCISE

Read the list of personal improvements that follows, and check off the actions you would like to take. Then write down a strategy for making a change in each area. Remember that the first step in making a positive change is recognizing a problem. The next step is creating a specific plan to remedy it. (You may need additional space to develop your plans.)

Take a look at these four examples of personal improvement strategies:

6. Speak more clearly.

Read the front page of the newspaper aloud into a tape recorder for fifteen minutes each day. Listen to the tape alone, or enlist the help of a partner. Try to improve your diction, rate of speed, and pronunciation.

12. Become more outgoing.

Join a professional organization. Attend meetings regularly, and make a point of speaking with three individuals each time.

14. Improve computer skills.

Add one small, measurable skill to your computer expertise each week. Learn to do spreadsheets, or attempt an advanced word-processing program. Start where you feel comfortable, and visit your local college's learning center, community education division, or adult-education class to get more help.

15. Improve writing ability.

Keep a journal. Free-write in it for at least twenty minutes each day. Later, choose a piece to revise and polish as a completed essay.

Personal Improvements   **_Strategy_**

1. Exercise more.   _____

2. Lose weight.   _____

3. Improve my posture.   _____

4. Smile more. _____

5. Upgrade my wardrobe. _____

6. Speak more clearly. _____

7. Clean up my language. _____

8. Stop smoking. _____

9. Become a better listener. _____

10. Improve my manners. _____

11. Pay more attention to
personal hygiene. _____

12. Become more outgoing. _____

13. Other: _____ _____

Professional Improvements   **Strategy**

14. Improve computer skills. _____

15. Improve writing ability _____

16. Improve public-speaking
skills. _____

17. Improve technical skills. _____

18. Other: _____ _____

Evaluate Your Priorities

As you progress in your career, moving from your first job up the ladder of success, you may find that your priorities change. They may be influenced by such variables as your economic needs, marital status, career goals, desire for personal time, and family needs.

Take a moment to consider your priorities in life. For example, if you're seeking your first job, your goal may be to obtain a position that gives you good training and serves as a steppingstone to more advanced positions. If you have young children, you may prefer a job that does not require any overtime or weekend hours so that you can spend more time with your family.

EXERCISE

Look over the following list of job and personal variables. In the left-hand column, number them in order of your current priorities. Renumber them in the right-hand column, based on your anticipated priorities five or ten years down the road.

Priorities Now	Job and Personal Variables	Priorities in 5 to 10 Years
_____	Salary	_____
_____	Family (children/spouse/parents)	_____
_____	Personal time	_____
_____	Job location	_____
_____	Work-related travel	_____
_____	Potential for advancement	_____
_____	Commuting time	_____
_____	Friendly coworkers/boss	_____
_____	Job responsibilities	_____
_____	Personal hobbies	_____
_____	Prestige	_____
_____	Benefits	_____
_____	Vacation time	_____
_____	Retirement plan	_____
_____	Security/stability	_____
_____	Personal growth/fulfillment	_____
_____	Exposure to new skills	_____

Choose the Right Job for You

As you embark on your job hunt, it's important that you clarify your thoughts about the type of position you might like and the kind of company for which you'd like to work. Once you've answered these questions, you'll be better prepared to market yourself and to find jobs that most appeal to you.

EXERCISE Answer the following questions. Keep your answers, and refer back to them when evaluating a particular position, to see if it meets your desires.

1. I want to work for a company with
  ❑ under 10 employees.
  ❑ under 100 employees.
  ❑ several hundred employees.
  ❑ several thousand employees.

2. It's important for me to be in a position with potential for advancement.
  ❑ True   ❑ False

3. I want a job that requires
  ❑ a lot of creativity.
  ❑ some creativity.
  ❑ no creativity.

4. I want a position with
  ❑ a lot of responsibility.
  ❑ minimum responsibility.

5. I want a job with the following hours:
  ❑ nine to five.
  ❑ part-time.
  ❑ flexible scheduling.
  ❑ potential for overtime.

6. I want to work for a company that
  ❑ promotes from within.
  ❑ brings in new people regularly.

7. In doing my job, I think I would like to
  ❑ juggle a variety of responsibilities.
  ❑ be responsible for one main function.

8. I would like a job that involves working with
  ❑ people.
  ❑ data.
  ❑ products.

9. I would like to work for a
  ❑ public company.
  ❑ private company.

10. I want to work for a company that is
  ❑ growing rapidly.
  ❑ maintaining its status quo.

11. I want to work for a company located
  ❑ within walking distance of my home.
  ❑ no more than a half-hour's drive away.
  ❑ no more than an hour's drive away.
  ❑ I will relocate for a job.

12. I want a position with
  ❑ a lot of structure.
  ❑ minimal structure and an informal environment.

13. I like work that is
  ❑ routine.
  ❑ full of variety.

14. I enjoy working
  ❑ in teams and groups.
  ❑ by myself.

15. I enjoy working with
  ❑ my hands.
  ❑ my mind.
  ❑ both my hands and my mind.

16. I enjoy working with
  ❑ computers.
  ❑ machines.
  ❑ neither computers nor machines.

17. I want to work for a company that
  ❑ allows employees to dress casually.
  ❑ requires employees to dress up.

18. I want a job that has
  ❑ no stress or low stress.
  ❑ medium stress.
  ❑ high stress.

19. I want a job that entails
  ❑ no travel.
  ❑ some travel.
  ❑ lots of travel.

20. I enjoy work that involves
❑ talking on the phone.
❑ face-to-face interaction.
❑ mostly written correspondence.
❑ minimal interaction with coworkers and customers.

21. I want a job that requires a
❑ high-school diploma or equivalent.
❑ college degree.
❑ graduate degree.

22. I want to work in an environment that
❑ does not allow smoking.
❑ permits smoking in specified areas.
❑ allows smoking without restriction.

23. To me, opportunities for training are
❑ very important.
❑ somewhat important.
❑ not important.

24. I want to spend most of my workday
❑ outdoors.
❑ indoors.

25. I want a position that pays in the following range:

$ _____ to $ _____.

26. Medical benefits are important to me.
❑ True   ❑ False

27. I want to work for a company that encourages further education and offers tuition reimbursement.
❑ True   ❑ False

28. I want a job title with
❑ a lot of prestige.
❑ some prestige.
❑ Prestige is not important to me.

29. When I picture myself at work, I envision myself doing

_____

most of the time.

Set Career Goals

Developing a sense of direction for your career is important both before you begin your job search and after you've landed a position. By setting goals, you can work toward meeting specific objectives, measure your success, and achieve a feeling of self-satisfaction.

EXERCISE   Fill in the following blanks with your current goals, your goals for five years from now, and your goals for ten years from now.

1. Type of job you desire:

Current goal _____

Five-year goal _____

Ten-year goal _____

2. Responsibilities you wish to have in your job:

Current goal _____

Five-year goal _____

Ten-year goal _____

3. Skills you wish to master:

Current goal _____

Five-year goal _____

Ten-year goal _____

4. Salary you desire:

Current goal _____

Five-year goal _____

Ten-year goal _____

5. Other accomplishments that would help you measure your success:

Current goal _____

Five-year goal _____

Ten-year goal _____

As you brainstorm about your goals, it may become apparent that you need more information to continue. This is a good sign. If necessary, begin researching a few occupations to establish their potential.

List your questions about one of your potential careers here:

1. _____

2. _____

Write the questions you have been forming about other career paths here:

1. _____

2. _____

Try Informational Interviewing and Job Shadowing

Conducting informational interviews and job shadowing are excellent ways to investigate your career options. Both involve getting firsthand information from people who are on the front lines, and both can help you focus your self-assessment.

If you'd like to know more about a particular job, why not interview, either by phone or in person, several different people who hold positions in your chosen field? As long as you make it clear to the interviewees that you are not asking for a job but rather would greatly appreciate their insights as you begin to focus your job search, you should have no problem finding willing participants. Before each discussion, be sure to prepare lots of questions to help you understand the interviewee's daily responsibilities and identify the pros and cons of her job.

Or, for a more in-depth perspective, spend a day or two observing someone at work in your targeted field. A job-shadowing opportunity requires time and effort to set up, but it may be the best way to ascertain that your field of interest is truly suited to your skills, needs, and wants. Here's how to go about it:

1. Find a contact person who works in your targeted career field. Teachers, relatives, friends, and networking organizations may be able to suggest names. Your goal is to locate someone who is willing to "show you the ropes" and let you follow him through an average day and observe his daily work routine.

2. Make it clear to him that you don't plan to interfere in any way. Remain a silent, unobtrusive "shadow"; listen and observe. Remember, this is not the time to ask for a job, although you may want to make note of contact names for the future.

3. If you are persistent and savvy enough to set up a job-shadowing day or two, you'll find your efforts amply rewarded. The insight you'll gain by observing the workplace and employee duties firsthand will give you a real taste of the field and a sense of whether it is right for you.

4. Follow up your informational interviews and job-shadowing days with thank-you notes to all those who shared their time and expertise with you. Make lists of questions you still need to research, reevaluate the pros and cons of the career, and write down contact names that might be useful in the future. You may also want to check out the *Occupational Outlook Handbook,* available at most libraries. It includes detailed profiles of hundreds of the most popular careers, based on interviews with people in those fields.

EXERCISE

After you have done several informational interviews or tried job shadowing, write a brief summary of what you learned. In your account, be sure to answer the following important questions:

1. What were the duties of the position? _____

_____

2. What about the job appealed to you most? _____

_____

3. What aspects of the job did you dislike? _____

_____

4. What surprised you the most about what you learned?

_____

5. What further information do you need to decide whether this is a career choice you want to pursue?

_____

_____

6. Make a list of any contacts or job leads you received from the people you talked to.

_____

_____

Take a Career Test

For some career hunters, taking the time to complete an aptitude test or an interest inventory at the start of a job search can be an eye-opening investment in the future. The most common tests are the Myers-Briggs, the Strong Interest Inventory, or a combination of the two. All these exams ask you questions that gauge your likes, dislikes, and strengths. But remember, the tests are just another tool in your self-assessment process. They are not crystal balls that see into your career future, identifying the perfect job and guaranteeing success. Instead, they will enable you to narrow your choices by ruling out occupations that would be a poor fit. They may also point out career possibilities you have not considered.

Psychologists, outplacement centers, career coaches, universities, colleges, and even some high schools offer these types of tests. You may even be able to find versions of them on the Internet.

Call in the Professionals

If you've done a comprehensive self-assessment and feel you need some objective advice, you might consider working with a career counselor or coach. These professionals, who can be found on most college campuses and in most cities, can

A career counselor can help you identify your strengths and focus your career goals.
(© Kathy Sloane/Photo Researchers, Inc.)

help you focus your career goals as well as target appropriate employers. Consult your student handbook, an academic advisor, or your city phone book.

You can also find experienced career counselors on the Internet. Most of these counselors provide their services via phone and e-mail. Initially, you'll have to fill out a profile questionnaire. The results are then used to send you referrals for the career coaches who can best address your individual needs. One last piece of advice: Be sure you understand the fee structure before engaging a career counselor's services.

Targeting Potential Employers

Learning Objectives

In this chapter, you will learn to target potential employers—in particular, how to:

- Generate job leads
- Network effectively
- Track your contacts
- Turn dead ends into live contacts
- Recognize the three kinds of classified ads
- Make contacts at job fairs
- Research companies
- Conduct informational interviews
- Determine whether you should relocate for a job
- Search for a job outside your geographical area

Chapter 3

STRATEGIES in ACTION

Rachel had worked as a nurse for the same doctor for nearly twenty years. Now that doctor was retiring, and Rachel was being forced to job-hunt. Putting a positive spin on challenging circumstances, Rachel looked upon the situation as a chance to broaden her horizons. She thought she'd like to try working in a hospital environment rather than in another physician's office. However, she knew little about the health-care business at large and, more importantly, about the daily tasks of hospital nurses.

Believing it was imperative that she understand the role of hospital nurses before applying for a position, Rachel went to the library to see what reference materials they had. She also checked the Internet to learn more about the hospitals in her area. But Rachel thought the best information would come from someone with firsthand knowledge.

She decided to contact several hospitals directly and also some friends who knew some hospital employees to see if she might arrange a few informational interviews. She hoped that what she learned in those meetings would help her target potential employers and prepare her to effectively present her skills in an actual job interview.

Generate Job Leads

Often the most difficult aspect of finding a new job is lining up interviews. Many job hunters make the mistake of relying exclusively on help-wanted ads and thereby miss some important ways to help generate leads. Here, then, are some ideas for improving your chances of landing a job interview.

1. **Personal contacts.** It has often been said, "It's not what you know, but whom you know." The reality is that most people get jobs through personal contacts— also called *networking*. Get in touch with your friends (including old college buddies), former work associates, suppliers, vendors, bankers, doctors, neighbors, fellow professionals, organization members, and anyone else you can think of to see if they can offer any job leads. Don't forget to ask them for the names and contact information of any of their contacts who might be able to help you in your job-search networking.

2. **Informational interviews.** Perfect for the person just out of college or seeking a career or geographic change, informational interviews allow you to gather information that may prove useful in your job search. Choose someone who can speak with you about his occupation: what it takes to be successful, where the best-paying jobs can be found, how to break into the field, and so forth. You should also ask the person you meet with to recommend other people who might be willing to talk with you.

3. **Managers who just got promoted.** You can find the names of these people in the Promotions section of the newspaper. They may be building new staffs.

4. **Potential employers.** Sometimes it's worth the risk of rejection to call employers directly and explain that you'd like to work for them and why you think you'd be an asset to their company.

5. **A fax or e-mail.** If a particular job you're interested in calls for assertiveness, try sending a fax or e-mail, particularly if it will give you access to a decision maker and will allow you to bypass traditional gatekeepers like clerical staff and the human resources department.

6. **Growth companies.** Growth companies (listed under Growth Firms in the *Business Periodicals Index*) are continually hiring new people.

7. **Newsletter editors.** Most industries have newsletters or trade journals. The editors of these publications are often aware of jobs in their markets.

8. **Venture-capital companies.** People in venture-capital firms are frequently aware of businesses that are hiring, particularly for high-level jobs.

9. **Position-wanted ads.** Many newspapers and trade publications have special sections in which you can advertise for the position you're seeking. Briefly state your accomplishments and experience.

10. **Employment agencies.** Call employment agencies in your area and see which ones tend to fill positions in your field. Many specialize in particular professions. It is most often the employer who pays the agency a fee once an employee has been placed.

11. **Executive search firms.** Contact these firms if you're seeking a management position paying a salary of over $45,000. Write a letter that describes your job requirements, lists your salary needs, and details your experience.

12. **Job services.** Most state job services have a professional employee-placement division.

13. **Alumni placement offices.** Keep in touch with your college placement office, even if it's been a while since you graduated. Placement offices often learn of jobs that require more experience than that of the average graduating senior.

14. **Trade/professional organizations.** Join these associations as an opportunity to network with people in your field. This is a great way to make contacts.

15. **Check the Internet.** Many companies use the World Wide Web to list their job openings. In addition to the listings on individual companies' sites, you can also find literally thousands of classified ads on general employment sites. See Chapter 10 for more information about job hunting online.

16. **Use the Yellow Pages.** Even the phone book can yield leads. Let your fingers do the walking, then start dialing.

Finding a job is often a numbers game. The key to winning is having as many irons in the fire as possible. If you're participating in all these activities, you're more likely to find that perfect job sooner than you would otherwise. Networking, answering classified ads, attending job fairs, researching prospective employers, and conducting informational interviews are all part of the process.

Networking Chart

A large percentage of job hunters find jobs not through classified ads or placement services, but through personal contacts. Ask around. You'll find that most people learn of job openings through a relative, friend, or friend of a friend. Initially you may feel uncomfortable asking others for help in locating employment, but remember that most people are flattered to be considered a resource. Making the series of contacts necessary to find the ideal position isn't easy. You need to be friendly, persistent, and sure of the type of job you seek.

Begin by completing the left-hand tier of the chart on page 28. (You may want to photocopy this chart for future use.) Tell as many people as you can about the type of career you're seeking. If necessary, fill them in on your background and skills. Ask if they know of anyone who might be interviewing or that you should contact. As you learn of more people who could help you, add their names on the appropriate lines. Be sure to thank everyone who provides you with even the tiniest hint.

Turn Dead Ends into Live Contacts

There will be times when you contact someone (either by phone or in person) who is willing to be helpful but, unfortunately, has no job openings for you. Here's where an assertive approach may work to your benefit. Frankly, if you don't ask, you won't get. So go for it!

When there are no job openings within a particular department, use the following questions (shown here and at the top of page 30) to elicit more help from a willing contact:

1. Who else in the company might need someone with my skills and experience?

2. Does your company have any other divisions or subsidiaries that might need someone with my qualifications?

3. Do you know anyone in my field who might have a lead for me?

4. Can you suggest any other companies that might need someone with my qualifications?

5. Whom should I speak to there?

6. Do you know anyone at _____*(name of company you're interested in)*_____?

**Names/Phone Numbers/
E-Mail Addresses
of Initial Contacts
(friends/family)**

Names They Provide

Names They Provide

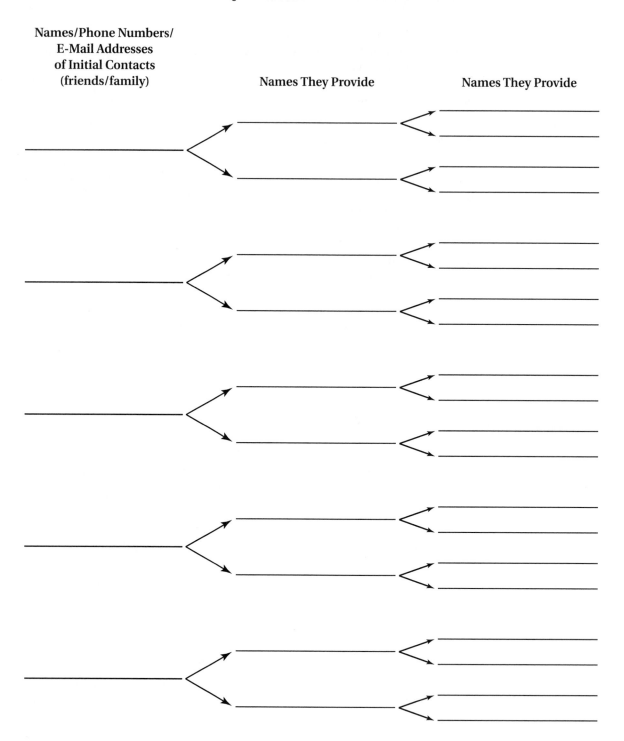

KEEPING TRACK OF YOUR CONTACTS

In generating leads, you'll develop a list of contacts. Photocopy this page for future use. Keep track of your contacts by filling out the chart below. Continue to add to the list as you make additional contacts.

Contact Person Name/Phone Number or E-Mail	Relationship/ Recommended by	Occupation/ Where Employed	Last Date of Contact	Suggested Next Date of Contact	Additional Action Required	Contacts He/ She Provided
Example: Mark Bergen (617) 555-9919	Coworker at last job	Accountant, Hyde Accounting	9/12/02	9/30/02	Send copy of résumé to him	Mary Smith, Telco (617) 555-1234

7. When do you anticipate an opening in your company?

8. Are you planning any expansion or new projects that might create an opening?

9. Do you have any part-time or freelance opportunities for me?

As always, be sure to thank your contact people both verbally and in writing for any help they provide.

Read the Classifieds

Classified ads in your local newspaper and in trade journals are an obvious source of job leads. Depending on the position advertised and the state of the economy, a classified ad can receive anywhere from a very small to an overwhelming response.

Types of Classified Ads

There are three kinds of classified ads. The first type, *straight classified ads*, run in small type, are under ten lines long, and are often categorized by position. They may or may not include the employer's name.

Display ads are larger and often provide more information about the employer and the job requirements. If responding to a straight classified or display ad that gives the employer's name, make the effort to visit the company's web site. It may include a more detailed description of the job opening; it will almost certainly provide information about the company that could come in handy when writing your cover letter or preparing for an interview.

The third type of classified ad is the *blind ad*. It indicates no company name, address, or telephone number. You respond by sending your résumé to a box number and have no way of knowing where your materials eventually end up. Many companies choose to run blind ads so their current employees and competitors won't know they plan to add to or replace staff.

Be wary of blind ads that appear repeatedly. They often indicate that the company experiences high turnover in the advertised position and does not wish to list its name each time it advertises for a replacement. If you respond to a blind ad and receive no reply, not even a polite rejection letter, don't be surprised. Companies that run blind ads often choose to reveal themselves only to candidates they consider hiring.

Setting the Wheels in Motion

If you answer a classified ad and are a viable candidate, you will most likely be contacted for an interview. Be sure to arrange to have your phone answered during all working hours, even if only by an answering machine or voicemail. If you decide to give out your cell phone number, always answer that phone professionally.

And don't forget to check your e-mail. Employers use e-mail almost as often as the phone to contact prospective employees. You always risk being passed up for an interview if the employer can't contact you easily.

Keep in mind that some newspapers post on their web sites more detailed information about jobs they've only briefly listed in their print classified ads. When that's the case, the classified ads are likely to contain a Web ID code.

As you read classified ads, you will notice that employment agencies regularly run ads to attract qualified candidates for placement. Go ahead and send your résumé if you are interested in the advertised position, but be sure to notice whether the ad indicates "fee paid" or "no fees." Either of these phrases means that your employer, not you, will pay the placement fee if you obtain a job through the employment agency. If this is not indicated in the ad, be sure to ask the agency about it. Although paying a fee to obtain the right position is not necessarily bad, you should be aware of the fee and exactly what service you'll receive for it. Standard fees range from several weeks' to several months' pay, depending on the agency and the caliber of the position.

Be especially wary of employment agencies that request an up-front fee. Check out these companies with the Better Business Bureau, ask a lot of questions, and carefully read any contracts you're asked to sign—before handing over your cash. If it sounds too good to be true, it probably is.

EXERCISE

1. Find the classified section of your local newspaper, preferably a Sunday edition. If you live in a small town, use the nearest large daily newspaper. Locate a sample of each type of ad: straight, display, and blind.

2. Check the classified ads for positions in your field. Identify at least two that you would consider applying for.

3. Select a classified ad that lists the employer's name. Locate that employer's web site on the Internet, and see if it contains a more detailed job description. If so, note what new information you gleaned. Do you think that information would be helpful if you were to apply for the position? Explain how. Also, does the Internet version of the ad offer a way to apply online?

Finding *All* the Job Ads

Beyond the Sunday newspaper's classified ads, there are many other resources to consider. Check out trade and professional publications, association newsletters and web sites, job hotlines, public employment-service job banks, online bulletin boards, and career sites on the Internet.

It's also a good idea to look through ads in fields other than your own. You might find a related position or discover another field that suits you. When it comes time to respond to ads, don't reply only to those that match your skills and interests exactly; respond also to any openings for which you might be considered—even jobs for which you're slightly over- or underqualified. Although all employers hope to find a perfect candidate, often they are forced to adjust their expectations to fit the applicant pool.

As you read the classified ads, take note of any companies that appear to be doing major recruitment. Often, they advertise only selected openings, even though they have others available. It could be worth a letter or phone call to the company's human resources department to investigate further.

Apply Liberally

Even if you're not 100 percent sure you'd like the position mentioned in a classified ad, apply anyway. The listing most likely provides only an incomplete description of the position's responsibilities. Once you "get in the door" for an interview, you can obtain more detailed information and make an informed decision. In some cases, you may even be able to tailor the job to better suit your interests and skills. The important thing is at least to get a shot at the position. To do that, you have to apply. Don't choose not to respond to an ad just because it uses a box number and does not mention the company's name. Many quality companies use this anonymous method to avoid being inundated with résumés. If the job sounds good, it's worth applying for.

If you see multiple ads from one company, apply separately to each position that interests you. The exception to this rule would be if you know (usually from a phone call to the human resources department) that the company uses a job computer to track applications. In that case, your résumé would be entered into a database, which is then searched as different positions open. The same advice would apply if you have been rejected by a company: Don't hesitate to reapply if a new position opens up, unless you know that the company uses a job computer for tracking.

Making Contacts at Job Fairs

"Too many people, too little time, and too disorganized"—this is how many job seekers view job fairs. But with the right preparation and a game plan, job fairs can be a great way to get in the door of companies you might otherwise never get to know.

Companies usually participate in job fairs for one of two reasons: to fill current positions or to collect résumés for anticipated future openings. Because they commonly spend hundreds or thousands of dollars to participate, the companies' presence alone says they are serious.

If you've never been to a job fair, here's what to expect. Each participating company sets up a table staffed by representatives. The representatives are there to greet you, tell you something about their company, and most importantly, assess whether you might be a potential candidate for employment. Companies with

the most urgent staffing needs often rent an interview room in addition to the table space, where they can do on-the-spot qualifying of candidates.

To find out when and where job fairs are being held, check with your college career office, keep an eye on your local newspaper, and visit the major career sites, some of which maintain career fair calendars or post notices about upcoming fairs.

To gain the most benefit from a job fair, consider these tips:

1. **Find out in advance which companies plan to be present.** Often the show's promoters print a list and make it available to the public. Ads promoting the job fair also will often list participants.

2. **Determine which companies are your primary targets.** Do a little advance research about these companies, and you'll make a solid impression when you talk to their representatives. Look up the companies on the Internet or at your campus career office, or go to the library and research them in back issues of your local paper, the *Wall Street Journal, Business Week,* or other business publications.

3. **Dress for a job, not a fair.** Conservative, professional attire is the way to go. Look upon the job fair like you would a job interview, and dress accordingly.

4. **Practice your delivery.** First, go to the booths of a few companies you're not interested in. Hone your presentation with the representatives of those companies and get comfortable in the job fair environment before moving on to your primary targets.

5. **Give yourself enough time to be thorough.** Job fairs may last several hours or even several days, so you should have plenty of time to accomplish your goals. Take the time to evaluate each company and to meet the representatives of your key targets. At the booths of the most heavily visited companies, you may have to wait in line.

6. **Bring many copies of your résumé.** Carry them in a folder, portfolio cover, or notebook, and don't be embarrassed to pass them out. That's what companies are there for—to collect résumés.

7. **Be professional when you meet representatives.** Treat your meeting like a brief job interview. Shake hands, state your name, and be prepared to give a two-minute introduction about yourself.

8. **Ask questions.** In addition to putting out information about yourself, job fairs are also a great place to get information. When meeting with the representatives, try to learn about their companies and obtain names of contacts to whom you can personally send your résumé. Ask the representatives for business cards so you can reference them in writing cover letters to the contacts (*e.g.,* "I met Sarah Jones at a recent job fair, and she suggested I contact you.").

9. **Make notes.** Bring a notebook or write notes on the back of business cards you receive, to help you remember useful tidbits of information about the company or the representative. Utilize that information when writing follow-up thank-you notes or future cover letters to the company.

10. **Collect company materials.** Most companies display corporate literature at their booths. Take advantage of this literature to learn about the company—its capabilities, corporate philosophy, and operations.

11. **Shoot for an interview, not a job.** Your goal at a job fair is to obtain a follow-up interview. Rarely do companies hire for professional positions on the spot. Instead, they contact their best candidates within a few weeks (sometimes months) of the job fair and schedule appointments for interviews at their company.

12. **Look, listen, and learn.** Use a job fair to gain insight about employers, practice your interviewing skills, and get a sense of the competition by checking out other job hunters.

Research Companies

One of the most important steps in job hunting is researching potential employers. The more you know about a company, the more specific you can be in your cover letter and the more direct you can be in your interview. Your research will also help you decide whether a particular company is one with which you'd like to be associated.

The following list describes some of the ways to research potential employers. Depending on your individual situation, some of these methods will be more appropriate than others.

1. **Check the Internet.** The World Wide Web is an excellent tool for researching companies and industries. Most companies today, big and small, have a web site you can locate using a major search engine or by calling the company directly and asking for its Internet address. Typically, company web sites contain information about the company, its products or services and key personnel, and any newsworthy advances or changes. They often list current job openings as well, and offer you the option of applying online.

2. **Subscribe to your local newspaper.** Keep your eyes open for any stories on companies you are interested in. Many newspapers also have cataloged archives in which you can find past clippings. You may even be able to access those archives online via the Internet.

3. **Read trade literature.** Most firms regularly distribute information on their new products, services, and employees to business-to-business magazines and industry trade journals.

4. **Learn about the company's competitors.** Call to solicit their sales literature. Use this information to learn not only about the competition but also about the field.

5. **Attend trade shows.** Many companies participate in local and national trade shows relevant to their industry. Visit their booths and ask about their products, markets, achievements, and future plans. You may also be able to obtain the names of the appropriate people to contact regarding employment.

6. **Attend meetings of clubs or trade organizations in your field.** Through these meetings, you'll be able to learn about the industry and about your potential employer. To find out about relevant associations, try the *Encyclopedia of Associations,* available in most large libraries. Some libraries allow you to access this reference publication online from your computer. Once you have the association names, see if they have web sites that can provide you with ideas for additional industry resources as well as potential employers and specific contact names.

7. **Purchase the company's product.** If it is not feasible for you to buy the product the company makes, try to locate an individual or a firm that has bought it and ask for input on the company.

8. **Ask suppliers and distributors for information.** They can give you insight into a company's business practices.

9. **Obtain financial data.** If the company is a public corporation, you can solicit an annual report as a potential investor. This document provides a wealth of information, from sales volume and product distribution to plans for the future. Much of that information may also be available online. (If the company is privately owned, this information may be difficult to acquire.)

10. **Call the Better Business Bureau.** It might be worth your while to find out if the company has had any complaints lodged against it.

11. **Visit the local chamber of commerce.** Local chambers often keep information on the businesses in their communities. Chamber employees might even be able to give you some personal insights if they have had an opportunity to interact with the company.

12. **Speak to ex-employees.** If you know someone who has worked for the company in the past, she might be able to give you helpful input. Remember to take this information with a grain of salt, because ex-employees' opinions may be based on their reasons for leaving.

13. **Call or visit your local library.** Ask at the reference desk how to go about researching a particular company. Librarians can often steer you toward a wealth of resources.

14. **Be resourceful.** Try to come up with some of your own ideas or contacts for getting information about the companies you are interested in.

Effective Networking

Good networking is about building relationships. The more people you know, the more connected you will be in your field. Connected people learn about job openings earlier, meet more people at a high level, and generally know more about their industries. Furthermore, connected people are more valuable to their future employers because they keep current on the developments and players in their field. Here's how to approach networking:

- Choose a goal or identify a target industry or employer. People won't be able to help you if you can't tell them specifically what you need.

- Develop a long-term, career-building approach. Who is it important for you to get to know in furthering your career?

- Keep track of the people you meet and make an effort to stay in touch with them through occasional phone calls, notes, e-mails, and even holiday cards.

- Think of others without being asked. That's part of the give-and-take of networking. For example, is there a project someone may want to know about or a relevant newspaper article he or she may not have seen? Or could you help someone else with their career networking by making an introduction or lending your name as a contact?

- Always thank others for their help.

Informational Interviews

If you suspect that a certain career field might be interesting, but you don't know enough about it to be sure, an informational interview could be the perfect way to get smart in a hurry. It grants you immediate access to someone working in the field. What better means is there to gain firsthand knowledge?

Arranging and Conducting Informational Interviews

Through networking, cold calling, or personal contacts, find someone who works in your area of interest. Call or write this person and make your proposal. Explain that you are not asking for a job but that you would like to find out about his field. Ask for fifteen to twenty minutes of his time, and set up an appointment. Be sure to keep your session to that length. Listen carefully during the interview. Jot down a few notes, but maximize your time by writing out most of your notes and impressions after the interview. Have a copy of your résumé on hand should your interviewer request to see it or to pass it along to a personal contact.

Follow-up is crucial. Immediately after the informational interview, write your contact a brief thank-you letter expressing appreciation for the information and names of other potential contacts he shared with you. Within the next two to three weeks, call the person to say hello and let him know what progress you've made, particularly with regard to any contacts he gave you. Thank him again and ask if he has heard of any new openings you should pursue. You may want to touch base with this person every month or so to start your network and to keep your contact strong.

Getting the Most out of Informational Interviews

Although every informational interview you conduct will, of course, be different, there are some cardinal rules to keep in mind.

- Be prepared.
- Be brief and courteous.
- Do not ask for a job.
- Follow up with a thank-you letter and an occasional phone call.

Successful informational interviews can help you feel confident that you're focusing your job search on the right career area and that you're supplied with fresh, appropriate information.

To get the most out of an informational interview, you need to be fully prepared. Research the company and field through the Internet, your local library, or any other resource you have available. Prepare a list of questions to bring to your interview.

Don't feel strictly confined to your list. Rather, in the interview, pay close attention to the conversation and focus on the areas that seem most relevant and interesting to you. What follows is a list of general questions you can use to get started.

Sample Questions for the Informational Interview

1. Tell me about being a _____ (*name of profession*) _____ .

2. What do you do in a typical day?

3. Which duties do you like most? Least?

4. How did you get into this field?

5. How is this field changing?

6. How do most people prepare for this job? What skills are needed?

7. What are the entry-level positions?

8. What other jobs are related to this one? Are there any particularly interesting specialties within this field?

9. How do people in this position go about advancing their careers?

10. What education or training is necessary for this position?

11. What personality traits are needed to be successful in this field?

12. What salary range could a person starting in this field expect?

13. What individuals/which companies are prominent in this field?

14. Could you give me names of people I might contact about openings in this field?

15. May I use your name in my introduction to those people?

EXERCISE

Write a few other questions—either general or specifically related to your career of interest—that you could ask.

16. _____

17. _____

18. _____

19. _____

As mentioned earlier, you'll want to send a gracious thank-you letter after each informational interview. The following example may help you start your own draft.

118 Blue Street
Atlanta, GA 01112

September 4, 2003

Ms. Karen O'Donnell
Appraiser
Carver Company, Inc.
Atlanta, GA 01112

Dear Ms. O'Donnell:

I just wanted to take a moment to thank you for your time last week. I appreciated the opportunity to learn about your many responsibilities as a real estate appraiser for Carver Company.

As I pursue my own career in appraising, I will keep in mind the information you were able to provide me. Your advice will certainly come in handy.

Sincerely,

Susan Johns

Susan Johns

Sample 3.1: Thank-You Letter for an Informational Interview

Should You Relocate for a Job?

Depending on where you live, there may or may not be opportunities appropriate to your field in your geographical area. Many of the best professional positions continue to be concentrated in major metropolitan areas such as New York, Chicago, Boston, and Los Angeles.

When embarking on your new career, it is important to consider not just the type of job you want, but also the place where you would most like to live and work. You can obtain profiles of different communities at the library in books such as *U.S. Census Data, The Book for the States,* and *Municipal Yearbook.* Check the Internet for information about regions you're considering. If you zero in on a particular area, be sure to call the local chamber of commerce, which can provide you with literature—often at no charge.

EXERCISE   Answer the following questions regarding relocating for a position.

1. Where would you *like* to live for the next five to ten years?

2. How appealing are the educational, social, and cultural opportunities in the area?

3. What are the psychological costs of moving? Do you think you'd be able to adjust? Would you be leaving family and friends behind? What impact would this have on your family?

4. What do you know about the quality and quantity of career opportunities in the new area?

5. Would it be better to relocate now as you embark on your new career, or to wait until you've gained some on-the-job experience?

6. Would you be able to conduct a job hunt in another community?

7. Is there any chance you could work for a company and then be relocated, at its expense, to another area?

Answer the following questions to determine the financial costs of relocating. If you're unsure of exact numbers, guess on the high side to be safe. Take the total costs into consideration when deciding whether you can afford to make a move.

1. What is the cost of living in the new area compared to where you live now, and will you be able to find a position that covers these costs? (This is extremely important because of the wide variation in cost of living between locations. A "good" salary in Boise, Idaho, will not necessarily afford you a similar lifestyle in New York City or Los Angeles.) Include housing, food, parking, and entertainment expenses in your calculation. Many career web sites now include calculators to help you compare wages in different regions.

2. Will commuting costs be a factor in the new location?

3. What will it cost you to leave your current housing situation (i.e., breaking a lease or selling a home), and what will it cost you to get into a new home (i.e., security deposit on an apartment or down payment on a new home)?

4. How much will it cost to move? Call a moving company or truck-rental facility to get an estimate. Is it realistic to think that your employer (if you have one) might cover these costs?

5. Will you have any job-search costs as you seek a position in a new area?

6. If you have a spouse or significant other who will be relocating with you, what expenses will that person incur looking for work?

7. What are the costs of child care or schooling?

Once you have totaled your potential expenses, consider how long your finances would allow you to job-hunt. Unless you have a job lined up, it is unrealistic to think you could move to a new area and find immediate employment.

Long-Distance Job Hunting

The first decision you'll have to make is whether to job-hunt first and then move once you've found a position, or to move first and then job-hunt. Obviously, the better option is to get a job first. Unfortunately, it can be extremely difficult to job-hunt from a distance. Most companies have a sufficient supply of good candidates right in their local area. They can easily interview and hire local candidates and avoid the problems and expenses associated with relocating an out-of-the-area employee.

To find job listings outside your area, check out the Internet. Many career sites allow you to search want ads by location. Also, many newspapers from around the country post their classified ads on the Web. Of course, libraries are also an excellent resource for out-of-town newspapers and trade publications with classified ad sections.

If you must have a job before you can relocate, try to spend weekends and vacations in the new city. Do as much research as you can before you make these trips, and if possible, line up interviews. Be sure to explain to potential employers that you plan to move to the city once you are hired. It can take a long time to obtain a job this way, so be prepared for a lengthy job search.

If you relocate first, begin job hunting as soon as you can. It takes a while to learn the ropes in a new city, and you'll want to land a position before your finances run out. Consider taking a temporary or contract position to help you buy time; you may even meet a potential employer through such jobs. Then follow the usual steps in job hunting.

If you are looking to work abroad, beware of scams. Some companies advertise listings of overseas jobs and then, after you send in your money, do not respond or send meaningless, outdated lists of multinational companies.

Most U.S. companies looking to fill international positions hire from within. Because the cost of transferring employees across national borders is expensive—traditionally three to five times a salary—corporations seek individuals who (1) have the necessary technical or managerial expertise and (2) have a proven record of success within the company. Unless you have a unique skill, significant international experience, and the ability to speak a foreign language fluently, your best bet is to work for a multinational company, prove yourself, and keep your eyes open for in-house opportunities.

Relocation, both within the United States and abroad, can be challenging. But those who do it successfully can greatly increase their employment opportunities and accelerate the progress of their careers.

Have You Considered...?

Learning Objectives

In this chapter, you will explore different types of employment, including:

- Federal and local government jobs
- Positions with nonprofit organizations
- Positions with small companies
- Self-employment
- Working in an alternative field
- Further education

Chapter 4

Mindy, a recent college graduate with a degree in public relations, had been searching the classified ads for a month and had found very few jobs for which she was qualified or that interested her. She had applied to all the public relations firms in her area, but none had been receptive.

Then she remembered the feeling of personal satisfaction she'd experienced when a few years earlier she'd volunteered with an emergency-disaster agency after a hurricane had swept through her town in South Carolina, leaving many residents homeless. Mindy had found the work extremely gratifying. She had liked knowing that her efforts were helping people in need.

Based on that experience, Mindy decided to contact the nonprofit, public service organizations in her area to see if they might consider her for employment in their public relations departments or even, initially, for some volunteer work.

Federal Jobs

Should you consider a federal job? Absolutely. To leave out the federal government in your job search is to eliminate the nation's largest employer. The federal government has roughly seventeen million employees. That's more employees than the first sixteen of the Fortune 500 companies added together and over 2.5 percent of the nation's civilian work force. One in seven Americans works for the federal, state, or local government. And despite attempts at downsizing, the federal government alone hires seven hundred new workers a day.

Types of Federal Jobs

Federal employees do every kind of job imaginable. Among their ranks you'll find statisticians, accountants, engineers, pharmacists, lawyers, law-enforcement officers, social workers, economists, artists, researchers, bus drivers, teachers, and morticians. In all, there are more than a thousand occupations. Federal employees work in offices, warehouses, shipyards, national parks, hospitals, laboratories, embassies, military bases, and many other places all over the country and around the world.

Don't think that you need to move to Washington, D.C., to get a job with the federal government. Actually, only 10 percent of federal employees work there. Federal employees work in every state, although 35 percent are based in or near the following ten major cities: Atlanta, Boston, Chicago, Dallas, Denver, Kansas City, New York, Philadelphia, San Francisco, and Seattle.

College degrees are held by 37 percent of the total federal work force. Certain jobs require a four-year bachelor's degree, a graduate degree, or a specific educational concentration.

Why Consider a Federal Job?

Job security is a primary reason to consider government work. Federal employment is generally not affected by cyclical fluctuations in the economy. Layoffs have occurred in the past, but they are uncommon and generally affect relatively few workers. Excellent pay and benefits, as good or better than in the private sector, are another reason many people seek federal employment.

Finding Federal Jobs

The Office of Personnel Management has automated its application process. This means that job seekers can get application forms and information about federal job vacancies more easily and faster than ever before.

Several sources of information exist for job applicants. Each system supplies information on worldwide federal job vacancies and application processes, updated on a daily basis. You can access this information in three ways:

1. **A touch-screen computer found in federal employment-information centers, state employment offices, and some federal personnel offices.** This very user-friendly system features easy-to-read menus and maps to search for federal vacancies. If you find a job you're interested in, touch the appropriate box to print the job announcement right off the screen. The printout has the name of a person to contact for additional details about the job, basic qualifying information, and the salary range.

2. **USA Jobs by Phone.** This is the U.S. government's official phone source for jobs and employment information, at (478) 757-3000. Extremely convenient, the system operates twenty-four hours a day, seven days a week. When you call, be sure to have a pencil and paper handy so you can write down the numbers you must punch in to access the various categories of information. For each area you select, you will be led through an additional series of choices. Calls average about six minutes each. Keep in mind that these are toll calls. Federal job information is offered for the hearing impaired, using national and regional TDD (Telephone Device for the Deaf) job hotlines.

3. **The Internet.** *The Plum Book,* otherwise known as the *United States Government Policy and Supporting Positions,* catalogs more than eight thousand executive and staff positions. The book is released every four years in the weeks following a presidential election. You can go to the library for a copy or look it up on the Internet. The Office of Personnel Management has also put a version of the same information on its web site at **www.usajobs.opm.gov/.** Do a search for federal jobs using your Internet browser, and you may stumble onto additional useful information.

Consider working for the United States government. One in seven Americans is employed by federal, state, or local governments. Their ranks include every type of job imaginable. (© David Ball/Corbis Stock Market)

Check Out Local Government Positions, Too

Over ten million people, more than half of all government workers, are employed in local government positions. Some of the segments within local government are: county government, school districts, fire and police districts, and park districts. The turnover rate for local government positions averages a steep 14 percent. That means there are lots of job openings at any given time.

Call your local state employment office or do a search on the Internet to learn about available positions.

Working for a Nonprofit Organization

Because more than 10 percent of the U.S. work force is employed in the nonprofit sector, you may want to give serious consideration to nonprofit organizations in your job search. Why work for a nonprofit company? Employees in nonprofit organizations often report a high degree of job satisfaction and personal fulfillment. They also say they enjoy the diversity of their work: Because budgets are often constrained in nonprofit organizations, one individual may be responsible for many different tasks.

On the downside, most employees in nonprofit organizations earn less than their counterparts in for-profit companies, and the pay gap between men and women tends to be more pronounced than in for-profit companies.

Working for a nonprofit organization can be an end in itself, or it can serve as a steppingstone to other types of work. If you're interested in a job with a nonprofit organization, know that opportunities abound. Because of their limited recruiting budgets, however, nonprofits often rely on contacts and referrals when hiring. The implication is clear: If you are looking for a job in the nonprofit sector, you'll have to do more than read the classified ads in the newspaper.

Begin by clarifying your goals. What issues interest you? Here are just a few examples of general issues addressed by nonprofits:

- homelessness

- religion

- hunger

- education

- diseases

- poverty

- the arts

- disaster relief

On behalf of what group of people would you like to work? Again, here are a few examples:

- children

- the disabled

- the elderly

- homeless families

- refugees

- the mentally ill

- abuse survivors

- unwed mothers

Next, learn which organizations focus on your issues of interest. Seek out directories of nonprofit organizations at your library, or search the Internet. You might also contact your local United Way chapter. Because the United Way disperses money to numerous nonprofit organizations, it often keeps a comprehensive list. Your local chamber of commerce may also be familiar with nonprofit organizations in your area.

Use trade publications creatively. Don't review only current postings for a job; check out old job listings as well, to identify organizations rather than specific positions. Consider consulting articles in trade publications to identify organizations that have just received additional funding or are working on a new initiative. Look for stories about changes in leadership. New leaders often make staffing changes and add new positions.

Ultimately, you'll want to research the issues, missions, and methods of specific organizations, asking yourself how your interests and skills might fit into those organizations' goals. Then, apply all the traditional job-seeking skills you've learned. Set up some informational interviews, begin networking, send out cover letters, and do cold calling.

If you have already identified several nonprofit organizations whose missions appeal to you, visit their web sites to view their job openings. Use a search engine to find those web sites, or call the organization itself and ask for its web address.

If you find an organization you feel would be a perfect fit but no openings exist, consider volunteering your time. Volunteering for a nonprofit organization is an excellent way to prove your commitment, verify your career choice, and make the contacts that could lead to a paying job.

Working for a Small Company

Although it may look better on your résumé and be more impressive to your friends and relatives to say you have a job at a large, well-known company, there are many benefits of working for a small business. First, you'll likely have more responsibilities than you would at a larger company. You'll wear many hats, which makes the job challenging, interesting, and a great learning opportunity. Second, you'll probably have more control over your areas of responsibility. There is typically less hierarchy with which to contend as well as fewer formal means of authorization. You'll be able to develop an idea and see it through to completion, probably without interference from numerous departments and superiors. Third, it's easier to get hired at a small company when you have limited experience. Presumably, there are fewer candidates applying for positions in small companies than in prestigious, big companies. Also, a small company may not be able to afford help with significant experience. They'll accept entry-level hires, knowing that those employees will need to do some of their learning on the job.

When you search for a small-company employer, don't forget to consider start-up companies. Although they may not offer job security (many new businesses eventually fail), they can provide an unsurpassed learning experience, not to mention a sense of pride in helping create something.

Starting Your Own Business

It's the dream of many: being your own boss and making lots of money. Of course, it's more easily said than done. But that doesn't mean you should rule out your potential for entrepreneurship. Consider the positives:

1. You're in charge of your own destiny. You make the decisions and don't have to deal with corporate politics and red tape.

2. You control the time you work—both how many hours and which hours of the day or night. (This can be a terrific perk if you tend to do your best work at odd hours or if you have young children.)

3. You have the opportunity for great diversity. As an entrepreneur, you may find yourself doing everything from sales, to production, to accounting—tasks that might otherwise be split among specialized employees.

4. To some degree, you have control over your salary.

Now consider the negatives:

1. You get to make the decisions, but you also suffer the consequences of those decisions.

2. Self-employment often means long hours because you are ultimately responsible for everything.

3. You have to be a jack-of-all-trades, overseeing every aspect of the business, at least during the start-up phase.

4. Because you are on your own, you do not have the support system of co-workers and an established organization.

5. Cash flow can be a serious problem for small businesses. In tough times, your salary is often the first expense to go.

6. You shoulder the stress over the business's success.

7. Because of the risks, job security is low, and the potential for failure is high.

Now take a look at the personality traits you'll need to be an entrepreneur:

- high energy level
- self-motivation
- comfort taking risks
- ability to make a long-range commitment
- enjoyment of problem solving

- ability to set high goals

- optimism

- ability to cope with setbacks

- self-confidence

- common sense

Do you think you have what it takes to make it as an entrepreneur? You just might if you have a marketable skill or product and the sales savvy to get customers. In fact, new businesses are being started at an incredible rate. The increase in the number of new entrepreneurial businesses over just a few years ago is due to a variety of factors, including (1) the trend of downsizing in corporations, which has pushed many midlevel managers and sales and marketing people into the job market; (2) minorities and women who believe they can get ahead faster in their own businesses than in traditional companies; and (3) modern technology, which makes starting a business cheaper and easier than ever before.

Although the types of businesses change with the economy and technology, the fundamentals of entrepreneurship stay the same. If you'd like to pursue starting your own business, begin by doing market research. This will help you verify that the product or service you have in mind is likely in demand. Develop a business plan and thoroughly investigate the feasibility of its implementation. Contact the local office of the Small Business Administration for information and resources for start-ups. Be prepared to work long hours and not to take a salary in the beginning. Start modestly and grow slowly.

In the United States, only 30 percent of all start-ups are still in business after five years. The more you prepare yourself and understand the challenges ahead, the better your chances for success.

EXERCISE

Answer the following questions:

1. Do you think you may have what it takes to start your own business?

_____

2. If so, which of the qualities of an entrepreneur do you possess? Which do you lack?

_____

3. What other qualities have you observed in successful businesspeople you know or have heard about?

_____

4. Do you think starting your own business might be a realistic option for you? Why or why not?

_____

5. If you were to choose to become an entrepreneur, what type of business do you think you might want to go into?

_____

Taking a Different Job Path

Having trouble finding a job that's in line with your chosen career? How about changing direction? Perhaps you have a secondary career interest or a hobby you could pursue in the job market—at least on a short-term basis.

Although taking a direct route up the corporate ladder to your dream job may be everyone's first choice, sometimes that isn't possible. A job isn't necessarily a career. And a job that isn't quite the right fit doesn't have to be a waste of time. You can learn from your surroundings, make contacts, and gain valuable work experience in every position you hold. Furthermore, employers are more likely to hire someone who already has a job than someone who doesn't.

Don't become stressed if it takes you a while to figure out exactly what you want to do or to obtain the perfect job. You may have several jobs before you find one that is your passion. And you'll quickly discover what you don't want to do. Talk with anyone who has been in the working world for more than a few years, and ask them about their first jobs. Although they may recount some horror stories, most will also acknowledge the value of those early experiences.

Sometimes you can find a job that has an indirect connection to your chosen career—like the grade-school teacher who works in a daycare center, the landscape architect who works for a florist, the physical therapist who works as a personal trainer in a gym, or the chef who works in a grocery store. Other times, your first job may be a major departure from your career choice—like the actor who waits tables in a restaurant, the dental hygienist who works in a real estate office, or the paralegal who works for a stock brokerage firm.

Remember that first jobs are not likely to be where you will spend the rest of your career. During the time you're working in your less-than-perfect job, you can always continue to search for a position in your field, all while earning an income and learning something new.

EXERCISE

1. Briefly describe your dream job. _____

    _____

2. List at least two directions outside your primary career choice that you
   would consider for employment, at least on a short-term basis. To develop
   this answer, think of your minor in college, favorite elective classes, hobbies,
   clubs you belong to, and any special talents you have.

    _____

    _____

3. Read through the Sunday classified section of your daily newspaper, and
   circle at least two positions outside your chosen career that sound interesting
   to you.

    _____

    _____

Now you can decide whether the time is right for you to apply for those jobs you
selected out of the newspaper or to employ some of the other job-hunting techniques described in this book to help you find a position outside your primary
career choice.

Further Education

One of the most valuable assets to today's employers is an employee who has
demonstrated the ability to learn and to continue learning. Perhaps your immediate future will have you sitting in a classroom instead of a boardroom.

Although many recent graduates shudder at the thought of spending another
minute doing homework, further education or training could be an essential
element of your job search. Just be certain you're not choosing to continue your
education simply to avoid the potential rejection that comes with job hunting.
Here are some questions to ask yourself.

1. Are you undereducated in comparison to others in your field? In some specialties, a master's or doctoral degree is common and necessary to stay truly
   competitive. Interview employers in your field, read the classifieds, and network to find out what it takes to keep up with your peers.

2. Are your skills rusty? Are you stranded in the breakdown lane of the information superhighway? Can you fit the most complicated thing you've written on
   a Post-it note? Perhaps now is the time to invest in yourself and your career
   potential. Many local colleges have refresher courses ranging in length from

an afternoon to weeks or years. Start with a simple goal, such as auditing a computer course at a local community college or adult education center, and see how quickly you can regain your skills and self-confidence.

3. Do you have a burning desire to know more about widgets? Or topiary? Or Shakespeare? Some of the most exciting and profitable learning begins with a unique, personal interest. Quenching your curiosities through a seminar, course, certificate program, or degree may be the beginning of a wonderful new career direction.

4. Will another degree or certificate make you more valuable to current or potential employers? Could you go even further in your current position if you took the plunge and signed up for a few classes? Would additional education or training enable you to apply for new positions within the company? Sometimes the only thing preventing an escape from a dead-end job is a few new skills. Inquire at your workplace to see what training or education is needed to secure positions that appeal to you.

5. Do you need to pass an exam, get a license, or get certified? Many professions separate the professionals from the amateurs by means of professional licensing exams or certifications. Yet many in those fields remain in lower-paying jobs despite having all or most of the skills to move ahead because they are intimidated by the rigors of passing a test or taking a course. It might be time to muster your courage and study for the big test. Take a refresher course or study with a colleague, if that will help you take the next step. Ask yourself what you have to lose. If the answer is nothing, then get started today.

Backdoor Your Way into a Job

Learning Objectives

In this chapter, you will explore various indirect approaches to job hunting, including:

- Holding a part-time job
- Working in a position remotely related to your main career interest
- Freelancing
- Working in an entry-level position
- Internships
- Volunteering

Chapter 5

STRATEGIES in ACTION

Carl, a civil engineer, had recently moved to a new area. Finding a job in his field was proving to be difficult. Unfortunately, many of the engineering firms in the region had fallen on hard times.

Carl interviewed at one company that seemed promising, but the owner said he didn't currently have enough work to justify adding another full-time engineer. Carl asked to be considered should the firm's situation change.

Upon returning home, however, Carl came up with another idea. Why not see if the company would offer him some part-time or freelance work? That would get him in the door and make him a top candidate when a full-time position opened up. In the meantime, it would allow him to pursue other potential jobs while earning some income.

Carl figured the solution might appeal to the owner because it would allow the firm to take on more work without the long-term commitment and costly benefits due a full-time employee. Furthermore, it would give both Carl and the employer the opportunity to see if Carl's skills and personality were a fit with the company. Carl decided to put his suggestion in writing and to include it in a brief letter thanking the owner for the interview.

Taking an Indirect Approach to Job Hunting

It is sometimes difficult for first-time job hunters to obtain a position in their field, or even to decide what position they want. If you fall into this category, you may want to consider a less direct approach to job hunting, such as working at a part-time job or a related job in your field; taking an entry-level position; or doing temporary work, freelancing, an internship, or volunteer work.

Part-Time Jobs

It would be great if, before you graduated, you had employers begging you to come work for them. You could name your salary and your terms. And you'd be doing the job you always dreamed of. Unfortunately, for most of us, that's not the case. If finding your dream job isn't as easy as you thought, you might consider another tactic—getting a part-time job in your field, even if it's in addition to another full-time job outside your field that you hold simply to earn an adequate income.

Second jobs are becoming common in today's labor market. They provide a means to supplement income, explore a career, establish a backup job for security, or prepare to segue to something more fulfilling. Even if it isn't a position you'd want on a permanent basis, it can flesh out your résumé and help you gain contacts.

If you're hoping to become a teacher but full-time teaching positions are few and far between, consider signing on as a substitute. Chances are, the income from substitute teaching won't be enough for you to live on, but when combined with another job, it could help you get by. Best of all, you would be gaining experience in your field and making contacts. When a full-time teaching position became available, you would be an obvious contender. As an aspiring teacher, you can also consider private tutoring. Or think about working part-time in a day-care center, after-school program, or recreational center.

If you'd like to be a reporter or photographer for a daily newspaper but are having trouble finding that first job, approach a small weekly or monthly publication as a part-timer. Once again, the income would be small, but the rewards in terms of potential opportunity and experience would be great.

If you're hoping to become a veterinarian, apply at the local animal shelter. If you'd like to be a corporate manager one day, start your own small business on the side. Maybe you do landscaping, word processing, disk jockeying at parties, or sales for companies such as Tupperware Company International or Mary Kay Cosmetics. The scheduling, organizational, and money management skills you would develop can be transferred to any job.

Having two jobs simultaneously isn't for everyone. It requires abundant energy, extraordinary time-management skills, and lots of "self" skills: self-discipline, self-sacrifice, self-marketing, and enough self-awareness to know your limits. To succeed, try not to think of your part-time work as just another job. Don't compete with or compromise any of your employers. And don't try to do too much.

Working in a Related Position

You may have your heart set on a specific job, but it's always worthwhile to take a moment to "think outside the box." That is, are there any jobs that might be related to the position you really want and that are more easily attainable?

For example, if you're seeking a position as a nurse, be sure to investigate all types of health care jobs. There are many technical and administrative positions available that allow you to contribute to a patient's well-being, even if in a less direct manner. From health information technician to home health aide and legal nurse consultant, health care jobs run the gamut. And many of these positions are considered ideal for long-term growth.

To find out about positions that might be related to the job you want, you should do several types of research. Read the classified ads in your local newspaper and those of major cities; speak to others in the field; peruse trade journals, particularly those that contain job listings; and surf the Internet for ideas. Working in a position related to your field, even if it's not exactly what you initially had in mind, can open your eyes to new opportunities while also allowing you to gain experience and make contacts.

Temping

One of the best ways to obtain a full-time job is to start off as a temporary employee. Such an opportunity gets your foot in the door and gives you the opportunity to prove yourself. More importantly, you can evaluate the company and decide if it's one you'd like to work for permanently.

Getting a temporary job tends to be much easier than finding permanent work. The easiest way to find temporary work is to register with a temporary service—or maybe several services. Having your name on file with more than one agency helps ensure that you work consistently and you have more potential assignments from which to choose.

To find the right temporary agencies, ask friends and networking contacts for their suggestions, or check your local Yellow Pages. Also, you can call companies you'd like to work for and ask human resources employees which temporary services they use. If you're fortunate enough to be in a field such as technology, accounting, health care, or sales, you may find a temporary agency that specializes in that area.

Next, contact the temporary agency and briefly describe your skills. Most services will invite you in for an interview, which consists of filling out a lengthy application form and meeting with a representative. Be sure to bring along a current copy of your résumé and any written references. If you're seeking a position in an office environment, you'll most likely be asked to take a battery of tests on the computer. Your keyboarding skills and knowledge of various software programs will be evaluated.

Be sure to specify for the representative the kinds of positions you'll consider. The better temporary services go out of their way to offer you assignments that meet your criteria, but you have to communicate those criteria early in the game. Unfortunately, most temporary agencies specialize in clerical or industrial jobs. Even though you may aspire to be a manager in a business, you're more likely to be placed in a secretarial job. Don't be discouraged. Remember that this is a temporary position.

During the interview, don't be shy about asking questions. Find out how the temporary service operates; that is, how the representative intends to match you with an employer. Don't be embarrassed to talk about money. Most likely, you'll be paid an hourly fee that will vary from one assignment to the next. Be clear with your representative about the pay scale you'll consider. If you have good skills, you'll be selected for higher-paying jobs.

Depending on the geographical area you're in, the specific temporary service, and the diversity of your skills, you could be offered a job immediately or not for months. Don't hesitate to call the temporary service on a regular basis to check on job availability. Often, it's the most motivated workers who are placed first.

Once you're given an assignment, try to get as much information as possible about it from the temporary service. In addition to the basics of when and where to report, ask questions to get a feel for the type of work you'll be expected to do.

At the job, adopt a full-time mindset. If you approach the position as though you are working there permanently, you'll make a good impression. A good attitude is vital. Don't expect to be treated like a savior. Most likely, you're simply filling in for someone who's sick, on vacation or maternity leave, overworked, or being replaced. Don't force yourself on others. You're not one of the gang, so don't take it personally if full-timers don't go out of their way to make you feel at home.

While you're working, keep your eyes open for opportunities for full-time employment with the employer. Many temporary employees do get offered full-time work if they prove to be capable and likable. If a position is not available, your immediate supervisors can pass your name along to supervisors in other departments that may be hiring or even give you the names of their own personal contacts outside the company.

While temping, don't give up your search for a permanent position. Try to use your lunch hour to make phone calls. Schedule interview appointments for after work hours or early morning.

Temporary work gives you income, puts you in the work force, and exposes you to potential job opportunities. It's a great way to learn about different companies and industries, and it gives you the chance to polish your skills and meet new people. View temping as a part of your education and the job-hunting process, and the experience will be worthwhile.

Freelancing

Many a full-time employee started out as a freelancer or contractor. What exactly is a freelancer? It is someone who is self-employed and sells her unique services to multiple companies.

The word *freelance* comes from the Middle Ages, when a knight would offer his lance and, with it, his allegiance to the lord with the most money. Today's freelancers offer their special skills to companies who pay for their services.

Companies hire freelancers when they need individuals with a specific talent, have a temporary work overload, or simply don't want to incur the expenses and responsibilities of full-time employees.

Typically, freelancing is associated with such fields as publishing and the arts. In today's ever-dynamic marketplace, however, freelance opportunities exist in many fields. Architects, writers, artists, secretaries, photographers, computer programmers, software engineers, nurses, and television producers are among the many types of professionals who freelance.

To be successful as a freelancer, you need a marketable skill and the persistence to develop a stable of clients. Sales is a major component of successful freelancing. As a freelancer, you essentially run your own business in which you are solely responsible for the bottom line. On the plus side, you have independence, scheduling flexibility, and the financial rewards of being your own boss.

Freelancing can be a full-time undertaking or a means to an end. It's a great way to backdoor your way into a full-time job. As a freelancer, you have an opportunity to prove your value to an employer. And you have a chance to get to know the people who can recommend or hire you when a full-time position becomes available.

Entry-Level Positions

Secretarial or mailroom work may not be your idea of the perfect job; it may be a way to land that first career position, however. Entry-level positions won't provide the salary or prestige you had hoped for, but they can get you in the door and in

Photographers are among the many types of professionals who can do freelance or contract work. (© Tom McCarthy/PhotoEdit)

sight of a position in your field. There are many stories of famous businesspeople and celebrities who started at the bottom.

If you've studied advertising, you might seek a job as an administrative assistant or account coordinator in an ad agency. You'll get to know the firm's clients, its methods of doing business, and the specific types of accounts it handles. Most importantly, you'll learn how an ad agency functions. If you've studied television production and aspire to be a director one day, you may be able to get a job as a gofer, doing whatever extra tasks need to be done, from photocopying scripts to taking phone messages. If you're a beginning attorney, you might find yourself saddled with paralegal tasks. If you've studied physical therapy, you may get a job setting appointments or greeting patients.

By now, you've realized that you're not going to start out as the president or chief executive officer of a firm. The first stage of your career development will most likely involve "paying your dues." An entry-level position, for which you may be somewhat overqualified and underpaid, could be a springboard to great things. Swallow your pride, work hard, and keep your eyes open for the next exciting opportunity.

Internships

Whether you are still in school or have already graduated, you may be able to obtain an internship in your field of study. Most internships are unpaid or include a small stipend. Some count as credit toward your degree. Although working for free may not seem appealing at first, consider this: Many top executives got their start through an internship program.

As an intern, you may be saddled with some of the less glamorous tasks of the job you aspire to, but you'll get firsthand, on-the-job experience. You'll make contacts and develop the skills you need to succeed in your chosen career.

Many interns are hired once a position opens up—there's something to be said for being in the right place at the right time. If an internship is financially impractical for you, consider arranging a part-time internship that would allow you to hold a paying job at the same time.

Finding an internship.   Your best chance of learning about internship opportunities is through college placement offices. They frequently receive and post notices about internships at local and national companies. In fact, many companies do their interviewing right on campus, using the placement office to prequalify applicants. Some college placement offices don't even require that you be a student at their school to participate.

Check out sources of internship possibilities on the Internet as well. Just as many companies list job openings on their web sites, they list internship opportunities as well. Some of the major career sites also include information about internships.

Don't forget to network to find out about internships. Many internships are not publicized. Rather, they are filled with people who learned of the internships via contacts.

There are also many good directories on the market that list internship opportunities across the country and even abroad. These books usually categorize internships by career field, location, and organization name. They may also offer details about duties, compensation, and competitiveness. Check your local library.

If a company you would like to work for has no current job openings, ask if it has an internship program. If so, you may be able to use an internship as a steppingstone to a real job. If not, consider sending a letter that proposes an internship, clearly explaining how the company would benefit from bringing you on in that capacity.

What to look for in an internship.   A good internship is one that includes more than "busy work." If making coffee is the only thing you learn while interning, your experience will have been a waste of time. Seek an internship that affords the opportunity to work on stimulating projects.

If your college internship coordinator does not do so, take the initiative to develop a "learning contract," in which you state your learning objectives and spell out specific tasks and responsibilities you would like to have. Put the contract in writing and have your internship supervisor sign it. At various points during your internship, refer to the contract to be sure you are meeting its criteria.

At your internship, try to find good role models. You can learn specific career skills from people who are seasoned and successful. If possible, cultivate a mentor relationship with someone who can take you under his wing. Finally, seek opportunities during your internship to broaden your knowledge of the field by attending conferences, seminars, and trade shows.

Volunteer Work

Although all students dream of earning "big bucks" when they graduate, depending on your career choice and the state of the economy, that may not be possible. In the first few years of your career, your focus should be on gaining valuable work experience, not earning a large salary.

One possible way to gain entry into your career field is through volunteer work. Offering your time to a company or an organization can get you in the door and enable you to explore career options. As a volunteer, you'll probably be able to set your own hours, which would allow you to hold a paying job as well.

Nonprofit or service organizations are usually the most receptive to working with volunteers. Some examples of organizations that often depend on volunteers are the United Way, the American Red Cross, libraries, and hospitals. Of course, every community differs, so you'll have to do your own research to find out about the best volunteer opportunities. Whether you are seeking a career in computers, public relations, office management, accounting, or health services, there should be some kind of volunteer position that would provide you with worthwhile experience and the chance to make contacts.

Even though you won't receive a salary for your work, you should not take your responsibilities lightly. To make the most of the situation, volunteer for an organization you are interested in or has relevance to your career. Work as closely as you can with professionals who can serve as role models for you. Seek out training within the organization. Every skill you master makes you a smarter, more employable person. Ask to be "promoted" to tasks of greater challenge so that your volunteer experience is filled with accomplishments.

Be sure to list your volunteer work on your résumé along with your paid jobs. Your achievements as a volunteer are significant. Potential employers will appreciate your initiative.

EXERCISE

Take a moment to consider whether any of the "backdoor strategies" discussed in this chapter make sense for you. Complete the following:

List your career choice(s): _____

Brainstorm some practical ideas for work that could eventually help you land your dream position.

1. _____

2. _____

3. _____

List some specific steps you can take to find any of these get-you-in-the-door jobs.

1. _____

2. _____

3. _____

Interview some people with at least several years' experience in their chosen career. Ask them how they broke into the field. Discuss the pros and cons of their methods of entry. Consider how you can apply what you learned from their experiences to your particular situation.

Part Two

GATHERING YOUR TOOLS

Preparing Your Résumé

Learning Objectives

In this chapter, you will learn to:

- Compose a résumé that accurately reflects the assets you would bring to a job
- Organize those assets under résumé headings and then organize the headings themselves
- Lay out the résumé in a way that leads the reader to the most important points while de-emphasizing the least impressive information
- Follow the basic rules of résumé writing, including résumé format and language
- Recognize the differences between chronological and functional résumés
- Handle gaps in your job history on your résumé
- Explore résumé alternatives
- Make your résumé computer friendly

Chapter 6

STRATEGIES in ACTION

Arthur's career history was varied and inconsistent. He'd taken time off to go to school, and he'd occasionally held jobs because they were convenient, even though they had nothing to do with his goal of becoming a computer programmer. Arthur felt that writing a professional-looking résumé would be a daunting task.

To help organize himself, he began by listing each job he'd held on a separate page. Then, for each position, he brainstormed every task he'd performed. He referred often to a list of action verbs to help jog his memory. Next, Arthur prioritized the duties he had listed on each page from most impressive to least. Finally, he was able to list each job title and follow it with a condensed, well-written description. Arthur went through a similar process when describing his education and the various training programs he'd participated in. He spent hours composing, and almost as much time paring down, the information on the pages in front of him.

Eventually, Arthur found he could fit the most important facts about his education and employment on one page. He rearranged the sections of the résumé, deciding to list a summary of skills at the top of the page, followed by the section about his education. He experimented with several different fonts and typestyles until he found one that appealed to him. He then showed the page to a few people whose opinions he valued—a former employer, a good friend, and a professor he'd had—each time taking notes on their first impressions and suggestions for improvement.

After making the final revisions, Arthur had a résumé he felt proud of, one that he felt accurately presented his experience and also provided a good starting point for discussions during job interviews.

How to Write a Résumé

How much time do you suppose the average employer spends looking at a résumé?

- fifteen minutes

- five minutes

- one minute

- thirty seconds

The correct answer is thirty seconds!

There is a lot of mystique and fear around writing résumés. Once you know the basics, however, there is no reason you can't create a terrific résumé that will capture an employer's attention during a thirty-second perusal.

Focus on the fact that your résumé is a tool to get you to the interview stage. It should present a concise, positive picture of your career goal, your education, and your experience. It should not include every detail of your professional life; rather, it should offer a condensed version of your educational and employment history.

Check Your Résumé Savvy

True or False?

_____ **1.** It is never acceptable to use lime green résumé paper.

_____ **2.** One of the most effective ways to draw attention to a certain part of your résumé is to leave space around it.

_____ **3.** The most important thing an employer should remember after reading your résumé is your experience.

_____ **4.** The descriptions of skills listed in résumés must be written in complete sentences.

_____ **5.** If your health is excellent, you should mention that fact at the top of your résumé.

Multiple Choice

1. Résumé software can
   a. create a generic-looking résumé.
   b. be a good starting point when drafting a résumé.
   c. be customized for different employers.
   d. do all of the above.

2. When the job experience section of a résumé is constructed to highlight the dates of the applicant's employment, the format is called a(n)
   a. functional résumé.
   b. chronological résumé.
   c. abstract résumé.
   d. electronic résumé.

3. An applicant's high school should be listed on the résumé if
   a. the applicant has not yet been accepted into a college or university.
   b. the applicant graduated two to three years ago.
   c. the applicant has demonstrated some exceptional skill or talent during high school.
   d. all of the above conditions apply.

4. As a rule, the résumé of a person with less than five years' full-time work experience should be
   a. one page long.
   b. two pages long.
   c. three pages long.
   d. written in paragraph form to expand upon the limited experience.

5. The average employer looks at a résumé for
   a. fifteen minutes.
   b. five minutes.
   c. one minute.
   d. thirty seconds.

The answers to these questions are given next. Expanded explanations of the correct answers can be found throughout this chapter. Some responses may surprise you, but they all should help you focus your reading on résumé preparation.

Answers to the Check Your Résumé Savvy Quiz

True or False?

1. *False.* In certain highly creative fields, outrageous résumés are acceptable and may even be welcome. However, most traditional, conservative professions require a traditional résumé.

2. *True.* Sometimes less is more. Try not to overwhelm your reader with an overly "busy" résumé, full of bold print or crammed with many different fonts and excessive graphics. Use a few tools judiciously to carefully call your reader's attention to the key headings, job titles, or dates you wish to highlight.

3. *False.* The most important fact an employer needs to keep in mind after reading your résumé is your name. Without that recollection, all the other information is useless.

4. *False.* A successful résumé is designed to convey the most relevant information in the most condensed format possible. For this reason, it is important to use telegraphic phrases, starting with carefully chosen action verbs, to describe your skills.

5. *False.* Years ago, listing one's health as "excellent" was an accepted résumé practice. These days, this phrase is unnecessary.

Multiple Choice

1. *d.* Some novice job hunters become so enamored of new job-hunting technology that they forget that creating a résumé that is unique to your skills, education, and objectives still takes work.

2. *b.* Be sure to examine many different résumé formats to decide if and how to highlight the dates of your employment experience.

3. *d.* As a rule, do not list your high school unless you are a recent graduate who has not yet matriculated into a degree program. If you had special work experience during high school, or if you demonstrated leadership skills or athletic or academic talent, you may want to include these facts on your résumé. Weigh the decision to list your high school accomplishments against the fact that they may flag your youth or lack of experience.

4. *a.* A well-written, one-page résumé is almost always the best choice for those with limited employment experience.

5. *d.* This simple fact highlights the importance of the "details" of résumé preparation. The lack of errors, the quality of the paper, and the neatness of the layout—all these take on unusual significance.

Basic Elements of a Résumé

The parts of a résumé should be arranged to illustrate your best assets. The heading and job objective usually appear at the top of the page, in that order. References usually appear at the bottom. If your education is more impressive than your experience, you might choose to put it nearer the top of the page, and vice versa.

Heading.   This is one of the most important elements of your résumé. Include your name (which should stand out above all else), your address (permanent and temporary, if you have both), your e-mail address, and your phone number.

Objective.   You might also call this section "Job Objective" or "Career Objective." Write a one-sentence explanation of the type of position you are seeking. Your objective should be as specific as possible and should not include your future career or educational plans. It usually appears beneath the heading.

In the objective, note a specific job title, skills you'd like to use, and the location or size of the company for which you'd like to work. You can (and should) change your objective to fit the job you're applying for. If you cannot narrow down your objective, omit it. Recognize that the inability to write a job objective is a strong indicator that you have not adequately researched your career goals.

Education.   Include all the colleges you've attended, their names and addresses, and any degrees you have received. It is perfectly acceptable to list a college or university, even if you did not complete a degree there. Give the dates you attended or the date you expect to receive your degree. In this section, you should also list any certificates you've received and seminars or training programs you've completed. Some people also note special honors and awards, such as making the dean's list. If you've been accepted at a college, it is understood that you graduated high school, so there's no need to list it.

If you wish to stress portions of your education that are especially relevant or current, you might also include a subheading titled "Important Courses" or "Relevant Courses." Under this category, you would list all classes you've taken that would be of special interest to the employer (computer classes are especially important). This section is useful if your education is more suitable to your objective than your work experience is.

Experience.   This can also be called "Work Experience," "Employment Experience," or "Experience and Skills." In this section, you list your previous employers, their cities and states, your dates of employment, and the positions you held. You may have to create your own job title if you didn't have an official one.

If your paid employment experience is limited, consider describing your volunteer work, internships, or practicums. List them just like your other work experience, but add the word *volunteer* or *intern* in parentheses.

For each job held, you may list either the company name, job title, or dates of employment first, as long as you are consistent throughout your résumé. The most important element in this section of your résumé is the description of duties, skills, and responsibilities of each job. You do not necessarily have to list job skills in the order of how often they were performed; it is preferable to list them in order of their importance to your current goals.

Summary of skills.   Some people include a brief paragraph or bulleted list outlining any special skills they wish to emphasize or that might not be apparent in the job descriptions. "Type 70 words per minute," "Thorough knowledge of Excel and MSWord," and "Fluent in French" are examples of phrases that might appear in a summary of skills. If your computer skills are extensive, this section is a must. It usually appears at the top of a résumé, after the objective.

Activities and interests.   You may choose to create a section in your résumé that lists your interests outside of school and work, especially if those interests dovetail nicely with skills needed for your prospective career. Some employers like to see that an applicant is well-rounded. Be aware, however, that others may view this information as frivolous or irrelevant. Be careful not to include any activity that might rule you out as a candidate.

References.   It is sufficient and customary to write "References available (or furnished) upon request." Be sure you can name three to five people who have observed your work habits and can speak about your character. Most people do not mind serving as a reference, but be sure to ask those who will speak in the most glowing terms. Compile a list of their names, addresses, phone numbers, and e-mail addresses. You might also want to explain the nature of their relationship to you. Employers who request your list of references are definitely interested in you.

Language of Résumés

The language used in résumés is unlike the language used in any other document. Your goal is to create a written summation of your skills, capabilities, and experience that is as brief as possible without omitting any of your strengths.

1. **Use action verbs.** Describe your duties with strong verbs—for example, *coordinated, delegated, trained,* or *supervised.*

2. **Do not use "I."** Each description of your responsibilities should begin with a verb.

3. **Use telegraphic phrases.** The "sentences" on your résumé should sound like the wording of a telegram. All unnecessary words should be left out. Words like *the, and,* and *so* often can be left out; the remaining fragment will still make sense. Notice the language in the sample résumés on pages 78–86. Each phrase starts with an action verb and ends with a period. For example, someone who has held a position as a customer service representative might write this:

> *Assisted customers with questions and complaints. Completed weekly reports. Provided material and assistance for production of monthly newsletters.*

Remember that it can be effective to list your skills in the order of importance to your prospective employer, rather than in the order of frequency of use at your former workplace.

4. **Use few abbreviations.** Abbreviating words may seem easy, but it's best to avoid this habit. Very few abbreviations are understood by all readers, so use only the most common: "St.," "Rd.," and the letters of your degree ("A.S.," "B.S.," and so on). If you are applying for a new position in a field in which you previously worked, however, you may use some abbreviations that are common in that profession. When in doubt, write it out.

5. **Use numbers that favor you.** It is fine to write "Completed opening and closing procedures of cash drawer." It is even stronger to say "Handled $15,000 in daily cash receipts" or "Trained 10 other employees." Being specific will enhance your credibility.

What Not to Write on Your Résumé . . .

Here's a humorous collection of sentences that were found on real résumés. (They were submitted by human resource departments from various companies. Reprinted with permission.)

- I have lurnt Word Perfect 6.0 computor and spreadsheet progroms.
- Received a plague for Salesperson of the Year.
- Failed bar exam with relatively high grades.
- Marital status: Single. Unmarried. Unengaged. Uninvolved. No commitments.
- Personal interests: Donating blood. Fourteen gallons so far.
- Note: Please don't misconstrue my 14 jobs as "job-hopping." I have never quit a job.
- Marital status: Often. Children: Various.
- Finished eighth in my class of ten.
- References: None. I've left a path of destruction behind me.

Style and Impact

Because an employer looks at your résumé so briefly, some of the smallest details take on major importance.

Paper.   The feel of your résumé in the prospective employer's hand conveys one of the first messages about you. Flimsy, shiny, insubstantial paper makes a negative impression. For this reason, avoid using onion skin or shiny photocopy paper. The paper you choose should be sturdy and professional—quality paper that has some weight and is marked "letterhead" or "résumé stock."

The color of the paper also sends a message. In most cases, you want your résumé to appear conservative and professional. White, off-white, beige, or light gray paper is fine. Some people choose to produce their résumés on light blue paper. Generally, the more conservative the business, the more conservative the color of the résumé paper. Hot pink might work well for a person applying for a position in advertising, but white would be better for someone applying to work in a bank.

Again, unless you're trying to make a special point about your creativity, the paper should be a standard 8½" by 11". Finally, match your résumé paper to your cover-letter and envelope stock, to give a unified, consistent look.

Format.   Because an employer's first glance will be a quick one, be sure that your most important points stand out immediately. How do you make a part of your résumé stand out while ensuring that the whole page is still easily readable? Think of the techniques that advertisers have used successfully for years.

- **White space.** Notice how the white space around a word catches your eye. Leave double or triple spacing above and below your name. Place headings in the center of a line. Put dates in a margin. Readers are more apt to read a page with lots of white space than one that is crammed with text.
- **Capitalization.** Use capital letters for headings or job titles.
- **Underlining or italics.** These are also a good way to make job titles stand out.
- **Bold print.** Boldface type can add a nice touch to your name.
- **Stars and bullets.** Stars and bullets help draw the eye to items in a list.

Whatever techniques you use to organize and highlight your résumé, be sure your layout is neat, consistent, and appealing to the eye. Study as many different résumés as you can to discover styles that appeal to you.

EXERCISE   ## Format Focus

Gather six to ten different résumés from classmates, friends, relatives, or coworkers. Study each one for only thirty seconds, perhaps even holding it at arm's length. After you glance at the résumé, put it out of sight and try to recall phrases or headings.

What is your general impression of the résumé (and job candidate), and what adjectives would you use to describe it?

After you've looked at all the résumés, answer the following questions: Which one seems the most professional? Which is easiest to read? Finally, which gives you the best impression of the candidate? This exercise often helps job hunters quickly find an appealing résumé layout.

Résumé Dos and Don'ts

Do

1. Use the best paper you can find (résumé, cover-letter, and envelope paper should match).

2. Use strong action verbs to describe your skills (see pages 74–75 for a complete listing).

3. List all your accomplishments, including important courses, volunteer work, internships, relevant interests, and professional affiliations.

4. Arrange your résumé to show off your assets. Which heading should go first? Education? Experience?

5. Make it perfect. This is a cardinal rule of résumé writing.

6. Keep the résumé to one page, two if you've had extensive experience.

7. Use telegraphic phrases.

8. Proofread carefully. Ensure that your grammar and spelling are impeccable. Also, ask a friend to proofread it for you, as it's sometimes hard to find your own mistakes.

9. Consider having your résumé professionally typed and printed.

10. Experiment with different formats and layouts. Are your skills best highlighted using the functional or the chronological format (see page 77)?

Don't

1. Exceed one page, unless you've had the experience to merit the additional pages. (Many employers only look at the first page anyway.)

2. Be wordy.

3. Use "I."

4. Use abbreviations, except for the most common ones.

5. Handwrite your résumé or cover letter.

6. Use unusual paper, type, ink, or formats unless you're trying to make a special statement about your creativity.

Arrange your résumé to show off your assets. Experiment with different formats and layouts to determine the best presentation.
(© David Young-Wolff/ PhotoEdit)

7. Include any personal data such as height, weight, or marital status. If this information is pertinent to the duties of the job, the employer will request it later.

8. Include any information that could possibly eliminate you as a candidate. Be especially careful to omit information about your religious or political affiliations.

9. Ruin a beautiful résumé by using a low-quality printer or reproducing it on a dirty copier. Take a moment to clean the copier glass to prevent blotches on your final copy.

10. Keep your résumé to yourself. Solicit opinions about your résumé from a variety of people you trust. Use their feedback to create a dazzling finished product.

Action Verbs for Résumés

Skim the following list to see whether any of these action verbs would be appropriate on your résumé. Remember that when describing your tasks in your current job, you should use verbs in the present tense. When describing previous positions, use verbs in the past tense.

Accelerated	Compiled	Drafted	Hired
Accomplished	Completed	Earned	Identified
Achieved	Composed	Edited	Illustrated
Acquired	Compressed	Eliminated	Implemented
Acted as	Computed	Employed	Improved
Activated	Conceived	Enacted	Improvised
Adapted	Conceptualized	Encouraged	Increased
Addressed	Condensed	Enforced	Influenced
Administered	Conducted	Engineered	Informed
Advanced	Conferred	Enhanced	Initiated
Advised	Conserved	Enlisted	Innovated
Allocated	Consigned	Ensured	Inspected
Analyzed	Consolidated	Entered	Inspired
Answered	Constructed	Equipped	Installed
Applied	Consulted	Established	Instilled
Appointed	Contacted	Estimated	Instituted
Approved	Contracted	Evaluated	Instructed
Arbitrated	Contributed	Examined	Insured
Arranged	Controlled	Exchanged	Interacted
Ascertained	Converted	Executed	Interfaced
Assembled	Cooperated	Expanded	Interpreted
Assigned	Coordinated	Expedited	Interviewed
Assimilated	Correlated	Experimented	Introduced
Assisted	Corroborated	Explained	Invented
Assumed	Counseled	Expressed	Investigated
Assured	Created	Extended	Judged
Attained	Culminated in	Extracted	Justified
Attended	Cultivated	Facilitated	Kept
Augmented	Cut	Fashioned	Launched
Balanced	Dealt	Filed	Lectured
Bargained	Decided	Financed	Led
Bought	Defined	Fixed	Lifted
Brought (about)	Delegated	Focused	Located
Budgeted	Demonstrated	Followed (up)	Logged
Built	Designed	Forecasted	Lowered
Calculated	Detected	Formed	Maintained
Chaired	Determined	Formulated	Managed
Charted	Developed	Founded	Marketed
Clarified	Devised	Functioned	Mastered
Classified	Diagnosed	Gained	Mediated
Coached	Directed	Gathered	Minimized
Collected	Discovered	Generated	Modeled
Commanded	Dispensed	Governed	Modified
Commended	Displayed	Guided	Monitored
Communicated	Distributed	Handled	Motivated
Compared	Documented	Headed	Moved

Negotiated
Nominated
Observed
Obtained
Offered
Operated
Optimized
Orchestrated
Ordered
Organized
Originated
Overcame
Oversaw
Participated
Perceived
Performed
Persuaded
Piloted
Pioneered
Placed
Planned
Played
Predicted
Prepared
Prescribed
Presented
Prevented
Printed
Processed
Procured
Produced
Programmed
Projected
Promoted
Proposed
Protected
Proved

Provided
Publicized
Published
Purchased
Quadrupled
Quantified
Questioned
Raised
Ratified
Received
Recognized
Recommended
Reconciled
Recorded
Recruited
Rectified
Redesigned
Reduced
Reevaluated
Referred
Refined
Registered
Regulated
Rehabilitated
Reinforced
Related
Rendered
Reorganized
Reported
Researched
Resolved
Responded
Revamped
Reviewed
Revised
Revitalized
Revived

Scheduled
Screened
Secured
Selected
Separated
Served
Serviced
Set (up)
Shaped
Shifted
Simplified
Sold
Solidified
Solved
Sorted
Sparked
Spearheaded
Specified
Spoke
Staffed
Standardized
Started
Stimulated
Streamlined
Strengthened
Stressed
Stretched
Structured
Studied
Submitted
Substituted
Succeeded
Summarized
Superseded
Supervised
Supplied
Supported

Sustained
Synthesized
Systematized
Taught
Tempered
Temporized
Terminated
Tested
Traced
Tracked
Traded
Trained
Transferred
Transformed
Translated
Treated
Trimmed
Tripled
Turned around
Uncovered
Unified
United
Unraveled
Updated
Utilized
Vacated
Validated
Verified
Widened
Withdrew
Won
Worked
Wrote
Yielded

Skills Identification

Skills tend to fall into one of two categories—abstract or concrete. Abstract skills hint at your overall potential; concrete skills are more specifically defined and serve to enhance your credibility. In your résumé, you should list some skills of each type. Examples of abstract skills are the ability to organize, quick proficiency at new tasks, and a positive attitude toward work. Examples of concrete skills are the ability to take dictation, knowledge of computer spreadsheets, and a typing speed of sixty words per minute.

EXERCISE

Make a list of your abstract skills. Then, next to each skill, give a specific example that illustrates your mastery of that skill.

	Abstract Skills	*Specific Examples*
Examples:	Good Organizational Skills	Organized a bake sale at my college
	Good at Managing Money	Served as treasurer of college chess club my junior and senior years

1. _____   _____
2. _____   _____
3. _____   _____
4. _____   _____
5. _____   _____

Now make a list of your concrete skills, such as your familiarity with computer programs, and other specific talents you've developed and specialties you've acquired.

Concrete Skills

1. _____
2. _____
3. _____
4. _____
5. _____

Review your lists of abstract and concrete skills. Place check marks by the ones you think are worth including in your résumé. Refer back to this page when you write your résumé.

Types of Résumés

As you assemble your résumé, you'll need to decide which of the two formats described in the following sections best highlights your strong points. Each type of résumé is more appropriate in certain situations, and both are equally acceptable, although the chronological résumé is more common.

The Chronological Résumé

The chronological résumé highlights the sequence of jobs the applicant has held. The "Experience" section lists jobs in order of dates, giving the most recent position first. After you've listed each employer, city, state, and job title, write a brief job description, using strong action words. You may place the dates in the left margin or after each job description, depending on how much you want to highlight them. Be sure you present dates consistently throughout your résumé; conventions might be "5/03–present," "May 2003–present," or "2003–present." A chronological résumé is best for those who

- have progressed consistently toward their job objective. For example, this format would highlight a job hunter's progression from a clerical, to a supervisory, and then to an upper-managerial position, because the job titles and dates of employment would be clearly listed down the left side of the résumé.

- have no gaps in their job history and want to stress the fact that they have been continuously employed.

The Functional Résumé

The functional résumé stresses skills, not dates. A clear job objective at the top of the résumé is followed by a "Skills" section. Three or four broad skill areas are identified, each of which relates to the job objective. For example, if your job objective states, "Seeking a position as an office manager," you would create such categories as "Office Skills," "Managerial Skills," and "Organizational Skills." In each category, you would describe how you have demonstrated those skills in previous jobs, drawing on your experience from all the positions you've held, paid and unpaid. A functional résumé is best for those who

- have held a variety of unrelated jobs. For example, if you have worked in a shoe store and a fast-food restaurant, a functional résumé would allow you to stress the fact that you've had experience waiting on customers, regardless of the setting.

- have gaps in their job history. Dates of employment are listed on the page, but further down; they are not the first thing an employer sees.

Look carefully at the sample résumés shown on the following pages. What do you notice first in each one? How have these job hunters magnified their assets and downplayed their weak points? Examine each résumé to see which format, chronological or functional, and which layout is best for you. Then, begin preparing a first draft of your own résumé.

Denise Mongan-Cordman

65 Longwell Road
West Hartford, Connecticut 06119
(203) 555-2642
DMC774@aol.com

OBJECTIVE

Position in technically oriented writing or editing.

SKILLS

Excellent writing skills.
Keyboard 70 words per minute.
Thorough knowledge of WordPerfect, MSWord, Excel, PageMaker.

EDUCATION

B.S., Journalism/Technical Writing, expected May 2005. Dixon College, Hartford, Connecticut.

Relevant Coursework: Advanced Technical Writing, Magazine Writing, Copyediting, Technological Reports I and II, Desktop Publishing, Introduction to Computers.

EXPERIENCE

2002–present

Publications Assistant, Alumni Office, University of Connecticut (part-time). Produce bimonthly medical reports; write copy and take photographs for faculty and alumni newsletters.

2001 Summer

Marketing Assistant (intern), NEC Engineers, Inc., Woodbridge, Connecticut. Wrote sections of proposals; copyedited manuals, brochures, and correspondence.

2000 Summer

Office Assistant, Department of Humanities, Dixon College, Hartford, Connecticut. Prepared mailings, updated computer records, assisted students with registration, performed general office tasks.

ACTIVITIES/INTERESTS

Editor, *Dixon News,* school newspaper, 2002–2003, Assistant Editor, 2001–2002, Copyeditor, 2000.

Secretary, Alpha Phi International Sorority.

References available upon request.

Sample 6.1: Chronological Résumé

SUMNER GOLDMAN

PERMANENT ADDRESS
(after 5/30/03)
21 Foxrun Drive
Bayville, Vermont 68725
(513) 555-0932
Sumnerg@media.com

TEMPORARY ADDRESS
(until 5/30/03)
Barnesville College
212 Metcalf Hall
Barnesville, Vermont 68711
(413) 555-3387

CAREER OBJECTIVE

Seeking employment as an officer in an urban police department.

EDUCATION

A.S., Criminal Justice (to be awarded May 2003), Barnesville College, Barnesville, Vermont. Dean's List, 2002, 2003. Degree also includes courses in Human Relations, Contemporary Social Problems, Report Writing, and Spanish for Law Enforcement.

Bayville Technical College, Bayville, Vermont, 1999.

EMPLOYMENT EXPERIENCE

2003	Barnesville College, Barnesville, Vermont. CAMPUS SECURITY ASSISTANT. Assisted Coordinator of Security with patrolling hallways, admitting visitors, and reporting incidents in residence halls.
2001	Parker's Photography Studio, Kearsage, Vermont. PHOTOGRAPHER. Photographed family portraits and weddings. Assisted customers in choosing among proofs. Worked in darkroom. Closed and secured studio.
2000	Smith's Burger Cottage, Barnesville, Vermont. COUNTERPERSON. Responsible for cash drawer averaging $2,000 daily. Took customer orders and delivered food.

PROFESSIONAL AFFILIATIONS

2002– present	Treasurer, New England Association for Students of Criminal Justice.

REFERENCES

References furnished upon request.

Sample 6.2: Chronological Résumé

RICARDO GRAVAS

15 Spears Street
Peterboro, PA 55162
(504) 555-9071
Rico@roadrunner.com

JOB TARGET

Seeking entry-level employment at a large hotel where I can utilize my computer and customer-service skills.

SPECIAL SKILLS/COMPUTER SKILLS

Fluent in written and spoken Spanish. Knowledge of hotel computer software systems.

EDUCATION

Fillmore Community College, Falls, PA.
A.S., Hotel Restaurant Management, expected 2005.

Important Courses: Front Office Procedure, Hotel Computer Systems, Hospitality Security Management.

EXPERIENCE AND SKILLS

Mile-away Motel, Falls, PA. *Desk Clerk*. Registered and checked out guests. Trained three new employees. Took reservations and processed payments. Assisted guests with questions and information about local sights. 2003–present.

Krystal Kleen Dry Kleening, Wenster, PA. *Clerk*. Assisted customers with problems and questions. Processed orders: Completed special-order forms. Operated cash register. 2001–2002.

RELATED INTERESTS AND ACTIVITIES

Member, Fillmore Community College Hospitality Club, 2003.

Certified by the American Hotel and Motel Association Educational Institute, 2002.

REFERENCES

Available upon request.

Sample 6.3: Chronological Résumé

Jie Chen

574 Highland St., #3B, Bolton, TX 87630
(304) 555-4671
EvergreenOz@excite.com

Career Objective

Executive secretarial position in a growing corporation.

Summary of Skills

- Proficient in WordPerfect and MSWord
- Experience with various spreadsheet and database programs
- Type 75 words per minute
- Thorough knowledge of all office equipment, including fax machines, postage machines, photocopiers, and switchboards

Education

Coleboro Secretarial School, Coleboro, TX. Executive secretarial major. 2003–2004.

ITX Industries, Brightfield, TX. Completed 15 hours of in-house training in areas of Customer Service, Computers in Business, and Telephone Techniques. 2000.

Experience

ADMINISTRATIVE ASSISTANT (Internship). Bruce M. MacDormand, M.D., Singeburgh, TX. Assisted physician with typing and mailing correspondence, newsletters, invoices, insurance forms. Answered patient questions and assisted receptionist with appointments and telephones. 2003.

RECEPTIONIST. ITX Industries, Brightfield, TX. Greeted clients. Answered phones. Completed light typing and filing. Assisted office staff with mailings and projects. Participated as an assistant and as a student in in-house training sessions. 1998–2000.

DAYCARE AIDE. Little Rainbows Daycare. Bellavista, FL. Conferred with parents. Planned and supervised daily activities and field trips. Assisted with meals. 1998.

References

Available upon request.

Sample 6.4: Chronological Résumé

Ember Newcott

337 Shasta Ave. • Rainham, IL 60649 • (208) 555-3820 • ENewcott@tec.IL.us

OBJECTIVE

To secure a position as an airline ticket reservationist at a busy metropolitan airport.

EDUCATION

A.S., Travel and Tourism, Illinois Community Technical College, Rainham, IL. Degree to be awarded May 2006. Completed courses in Domestic Travel Procedures (includes SABRE and Worldspan training), PC Applications, and Conversational Spanish.

EXPERIENCE

Office Assistant (Intern). Runaway Travel, Otis, IL. Assisted agents with arranging and booking foreign and domestic travel arrangements. Special assistant for Medco, Inc., travel accounts, serving all 4,000 Medco employees, including management and CEO. Greeted customers. Responded to telephone inquiries. 2003–2004.

Customer Service Representative. Spencer Gifts and Novelties, Charlestown, IL. Assisted customers with selection and purchase of merchandise. Handled cash. Maintained appearance of all store displays. 1999–2001.

EXTRACURRICULAR

Vice President, Illinois Community Technical College Travel Club. Arranged club tours to Orlando and Niagara Falls. Responsible for publicity and financial arrangements for both trips. 2004.

REFERENCES

Available upon request.

Sample 6.5: Chronological Résumé

Virginia M. Sheehan

2421 Bluegrass Circle
St. George, OR
(304) 555-1610
VMSheehan@juneau.com

GOAL

Seeking employment as a CAD Manager.

EMPLOYMENT

CAD Operator. Drawings Unlimited, Holiday, OR. Experience with AutoCAD R13, Data-CAD 7, and MiniCAD 6. Assisted with client conferences. Trained three new hires. Voted Employee of the Year for 2002. 2000–present.

CAD Operator. David White Associates, St. George, OR. Assisted designers with residential planning, layout, and structural calculations. Produced drawings both manually and electronically. 1999.

EDUCATION

A.S., Yeaton Technical College, Asbestos, WA. 2001. Graduated Magna Cum Laude. Important Courses: Computer Information Systems, Design Drafting I and II, Technical Writing.

REFERENCES

Available upon request.

Sample 6.6: Chronological Résumé

Philip Malo
75 Curtis Lane
Tilton, CA 96145
(858) 555-3640
Malo@earthlink.com

OBJECTIVE

Management trainee position in retail sales, using skills in design, administration, and public contact.

PROFESSIONAL EXPERIENCE AND SKILLS

Management

Coordinated operations, managed and assisted in sales at Peterson Stationery.

Managed small medical laboratory at Petri Laboratories.

Trained military personnel in hazardous-waste procedures at Pease Air Force Base.

Administration

Wrote and catalogued procedures for medical laboratory in Bow, CA. Designed new record forms, evaluated and carried out daily work priorities.

Coordinated numerous experiments from inception through subsequent interpretation and reporting of findings.

Technical Skills

Type 75 wpm. Familiar with most desktop publishing and spreadsheet programs.

WORK HISTORY

2003	Research Assistant—Petrie Laboratories, Bow, CA.
2001	Sales & Operations—Peterson Stationery, Concord, CA.
1999–2001	Hotline Volunteer—Women's Crisis Center, Generra, WY.
1989–1999	Family management and independent study.

EDUCATION

B.S., Retailing, Metropolitan College, Providence, CA.

References available on request.

Sample 6.7: Functional Résumé

Tyron Franklin

778 Sterling Park Road
Natick, MA 02134
(508) 555-9898

JOB OBJECTIVE

Bank teller in a large metropolitan bank.

SKILLS AND EXPERIENCE

Customer Service   Handled customer inquiries and complaints at brokerage firm. Educated and advised customers on new insurance products.

Sales   Solicited donations for renovations of community gardens.

Secretarial   Type 75 words per minute.
Experienced data entry clerk.
Recently completed coursework in Business Computer Applications.

EMPLOYMENT HISTORY

Insurance Agent	Whittemore Insurance, Natick, MA	2004
Office Assistant	Johnson Brokerage Firm, Stow, MA	2002
Medical Assistant	Sam Donagan, M.D., Gloucester, MA	2000–2002
Assistant Teacher	Wee Ones Daycare, Hyannis, MA	1999

EDUCATION

A.S., Business Studies, Merritt College, Boston, MA	2003
Certificate & License, Medical Assisting, City College, Boston, MA	2000

References available upon request.

Sample 6.8: Functional Résumé

Timothy R. Brock

4 Maple Street
Vernon, CO
(703) 555-0074

JOB OBJECTIVE: Daycare Center Assistant Manager

SKILLS

Curriculum Development: Planned curriculum units on Native Americans Studies, Forest Studies, and Dinosaurs for children aged 3–5 as part of practicum experience.
Wrote three children's books (unpublished) as part of Children's Literature course.

Art/Creativity: Planned, coordinated, and participated in creation of a full wall mural at Greater Vernon Boys' Club.
Experienced in introducing manipulatives, paints, beads, and cooking to children aged 2–5.

Conferencing: Observed children in Kids' Inn preschool center and prepared weekly observation reports to be shared with classmates and site supervisor. Discussed behavior and educational growth with parents of two young children under my supervision.

EDUCATION

Barlow Community College, Boynton, CO. A.S., Early Childhood Education, 2004. Coursework included:

Creative Development	Exceptional and At-Risk Children
Daycare Organization	Children's Literature

Completed 120 hours of observation and 150 hours of practical training.

WORK HISTORY

Counselor, Greater Vernon Boys' Club, Vernon, CO, 2002–present
Daycare Aide (practicum), Wunderkind Daycare, Clayton, CO, 2002
Deli Clerk, Shop 'N' Save, Vernon, CO, 2001
Child-Care Provider, Ms. Mitzu Park, Vernon, CO, 2001

RELATED INTERESTS

Big Brother, Big Brothers of America, Inc., 2001–present

REFERENCES

Available upon request.

Sample 6.9: Functional Résumé

Résumé Revision

The résumé on the following page contains at least a dozen errors. Look it over, and begin planning some corrections.

This résumé is clearly a first draft needing revisions before it is ready to be presented to an employer. In its current condition, it makes a negative statement about the candidate.

Try your own revision of this résumé. Practice with both chronological and functional formats, and experiment with the layout. See how you can improve Eva's chances of getting an interview; then compare your revisions with the two other versions that follow here. (Please note that you may have to be creative and fill in some of the details omitted in the original version.)

RESUME   3/28/03

Eva White
rfd2 box 199
Red Rock, Arizona

Personnel Data
Separated, 2 children
Excellant Health

EDUCATION

Red Rock H.S. 1999–00
GED '01
Attempted 5 courses at Mesa Comm. College

Experience

Schuylers' Dept. Store, 491 Los Nubes Blvd. Autusville, Arizona
(415) 555-6130
January–Nov. 1996

Part-time Assembly Line worker at Microtex Incorp. Carille, AZ 16 Industrial Drive 8/96–
now I make printed circuit boards and do many p-50 forms I also help QC when needed.

HOBBIES

Painting, voleyball, suntanning, biking, poetry, basketball, and all sports, reading, guitar, etc.
also a singer in the choir of Faith Christian Church.

Sample 6.10: Poorly Done Résumé

Did you notice the misspellings, sloppy format, and lack of information about skills? Pertinent information is omitted, whereas irrelevant data is readily apparent. The applicant's name is not especially noticeable, and there is no phone number or mention of references. The date at the top of the page is unnecessary. Also note the inconsistencies in the presentation of dates and the order of information.

By now you may realize that a good deal of work is involved in résumé revision. Although Eva's first draft has many errors, it is not unusually bad for a first attempt. The act of "diving in" and putting information in writing takes courage, but at the very least, it provides a place to start.

After you've drafted one revision of this résumé, compare your work with another person's draft. Do you agree with your classmate's revisions? What further changes could be made?

EVA WHITE

RFD 2, Box 199
Red Rock, AZ 66114
(415) 555-0938
Evawhite@longitude.com

Job Objective: Position as a medical secretary in a busy pediatric practice.

Experience:

2002–present   *Child-Care Provider.* Self-employed, Red Rock, AZ. Care for three children aged six months to five years. Plan and supervise activities and meals. Confer with parents.

2001   *Medical Secretary* (internship). Red Rock Pediatric Group. Red Rock, AZ. Assisted receptionist with greeting patients. Processed various health insurance forms. Filed and retrieved medical records. Assisted with transcription of physicians' notes.

1998   *Assembler* (part-time). Microtex, Inc., Carille, AZ. Assembled printed circuit boards. Cross-trained to assist quality control staff. Completed daily production reports.

1996–1998   *Sales Associate.* Schuyler's Department Store, Autusville, AZ. Assisted customers with purchases and returns. Trained three junior associates. Operated cash register. Managed cosmetics department in manager's absence.

Education:

2003   Mesa Community College, Mesa, AZ. Medical Secretary/Transcriptionist Diploma Program.

Relevant Courses: Medical Terminology, Medical Machine Transcription, Word/Information Processing, Office Systems Management.

References:

References provided on request.

Sample 6.11: Revised Résumé in Chronological Format

EVA WHITE

RFD 2, Box 199
Red Rock, AZ 66114
(415) 555-0938
Evawhite@longitude.com

Objective:

Position as a medical secretary in a busy pediatric practice.

Skills:

- Secretarial—Type 60 wpm. Experienced medical transcriptionist and receptionist. Processed insurance forms. Filed and retrieved medical records.

- Computer Skills—Knowledge of AppointmentBook software as well as various spreadsheet and word-processing programs.

- Public Contact—Assisted department store customers with purchases and returns. Confer with parents of young children on progress and behaviors.

- Teamwork—Worked closely with seven other employees on circuit board assembly line. Cross-trained to assist with quality control staff. Assisted store manager with cosmetics department in department manager's absence.

Education:

Mesa Community College, Mesa, AZ. Diploma, Medical Secretary/ Transcriptionist. 2003.

Relevant Courses: Medical Terminology. Medical Machine Transcription. Word/Information Processing. Office Systems Management.

Work History:

Child-Care Provider, self-employed. Red Rock, AZ. 2002–present

Medical Secretary (Externship), Red Rock Pediatric Group,
Red Rock, AZ. 2001.

Assembler (part-time), Microtex, Inc., Carille, AZ. 1998.

Sales Associate, Schuyler's Department Store, Autusville, AZ.
1996–1998.

References:

References provided on request.

Sample 6.12: Revised Résumé in Functional Format

EXERCISE   ### Résumé Worksheet

This worksheet provides an opportunity for brainstorming. Completing it will enable you to remember all your education, skills, and experience, and will lead you to organize your thoughts. Thinking through your skills should prove helpful not only for writing your résumé, but also during the interview process.

As in any brainstorming exercise, there are no wrong answers; include everything you can think of in each category. It is best to complete items 2 through 11 after you've let the information in item 1 sit for a few days. This will enable you to gain some distance from your work and make more effective revisions.

Before beginning, you may want to photocopy the résumé worksheet for future use as your career progresses.

1. Fill in the information requested in the six following sections.

   a. **Job Objective.**

      Career fields in which you'd be
      interested   _____

      Specific positions or types of positions   _____

      Skills you'd like to use   _____

      Size or location (*i.e.,* urban, rural) of
      desirable workplace   _____

   b. **Education.** Remember to list your schooling in reverse chronological order (most recent first).

      College attended (name) _____ (city/state) _____

      Degree received/date _____

      Relevant or important courses _____

      Other college attended (name) _____ (city/state) _____

      Degree received/date _____

      Relevant or important courses

      _____

      _____

      Additional educational training (seminars, workshops, extracurricular activities)

      _____

      _____

c. **Experience.** As above, list your experience in reverse chronological order. Include volunteer work and internships (and identify them as such in parentheses after the job title). You may need additional sheets to fully describe your skills.

Employer (city/state)	*Job Title/Dates Worked*	*Description of Skills (use action verbs)*
_____	_____	_____
_____	_____	_____
_____	_____	_____
_____	_____	_____
_____	_____	_____
_____	_____	_____
_____	_____	_____
_____	_____	_____
_____	_____	_____
_____	_____	_____

d. **Awards and Honors.**

Award/Honor	*Date Received*
_____	_____
_____	_____
_____	_____
_____	_____

e. **Professional Affiliations.**

Organization	*Year Joined*	*Position Held*
_____	_____	_____
_____	_____	_____
_____	_____	_____
_____	_____	_____

f. **Interests and Activities.** List all extracurricular activities, interests, hobbies, volunteer work, clubs to which you belong, etc.

_____

_____

_____

2. Referring back to item 1(c), revise your job duties. Reorder your skills so that the most impressive appear first in the job description. Use strong verbs to begin each sentence.

Position 1 _____

Description of skills _____

Position 2 _____

Description of skills _____

Position 3 _____

Description of skills _____

3. Using the ideas generated in item 1(a), write several one-sentence versions of your job objective. Then circle the one that is the most clear and concise.

a. _____

b. _____

c. _____

4. Review the previous sections. Cross out any mention of controversial, political, or religious activities.

5. Using the space to the left of each heading in item 1, number the headings in the order in which you'd like them to appear on your résumé. Remember, in your résumé, you will place your strongest sections closest to the top of the page. If you have a strong career objective, it should appear second only to your name and address. References are usually stated last. The order of the rest of the elements is flexible. Mark an X by any sections you would not like to include.

6. Now, prepare a draft of your résumé. Lay out the rough information you have gathered in this worksheet. Where will the headings be placed? How will you present the employment information? Where will you use capital letters, bold print, italics, white space, or underlining?

7. Show your draft to at least one other person who has experience working with résumés. A teacher, employer, or businessperson would be ideal. Ask the following questions:

    a. What does the person notice first? Is this what you had intended to highlight?

    b. Is your career objective clear? Is it too vague or too narrow?

    c. Are all your strengths included?

    d. Are the descriptions of your skills thorough, and do they start with action verbs?

    e. Is the layout neat and eye-catching?

    f. What other comments does this person have about your résumé? Would the person hire you?

8. Revise your draft, taking into account the feedback you've received.

9. Proofread carefully. Be sure there are no typos or misspellings. Make sure you have styled dates and punctuation consistently.

10. Print your résumé on a piece of plain white paper.

11. Proofread again.

12. Using the copy on white paper as a master, photocopy your résumé on good-quality paper of the type sold in office supply stores and print shops. Or, you may print directly onto your good paper. One other option is to have your résumé professionally printed. Although this is an added expense, it will help make your résumé look professional.

What to Do about Gaps in Your Job History

For a variety of reasons, many people have gaps in their job histories. Some were not employed outside the home after they had children; some took time off for travel, medical reasons, or soul-searching. There are also those who reenter the job market after retiring or after a long job search. In all these cases, job hunters may wonder how to express time outside the job market appropriately on a résumé.

If you are concerned about how to explain the gaps in your job history, consider the following suggestions:

- **Create a functional résumé.** Emphasize your objective; then list three or four transferable skill areas. Describe all the ways in which you have demonstrated those skills. Place your dates of employment in a section further down the page.

- **Write a chronological résumé.** Place the dates of your employment at the *end* of each job description.

- **Minimize the gap.** Give only the years of employment instead of both the month and the year.

- **Create a job title to explain the time gap.** Many people actually have done productive, albeit unpaid, work during their "gap time." Be honest but creative.

Could you call yourself an independent consultant? Family manager? One woman who spent years entertaining her husband's international business clients for weeks at a time decided on a title of International Hostess/Party Planner. Be sure not to overlook volunteer work or internships. Create a job title and put the word *volunteer* or *intern* in parentheses following the title.

- **Create new headings on your résumé.** If your work experience is limited or spotty, stress other strengths. Create categories for "Special Skills," "Awards and Honors," "Interests and Activities," "Relevant Courses," or "Additional Training."

- **Don't lie.** In an interview, explain any time gaps briefly but honestly. Remember, even a great résumé does not get you a job. *You* get yourself the job during the interview. In minimizing the time gaps in your résumé, your intention is not to deceive the employer but to prevent yourself from being eliminated before the interview. Plan ahead about how to explain the time gaps should the question arise.

FAQs for the Experienced Job Hunter

The experienced job hunter faces questions unlike those that challenge someone new to the job market. When writing a résumé and preparing to search for a position in a new field, how is it best to document an extensive, unusual, or complicated work history? What about any unpaid positions? What training or education should be included? Although the general rules of résumé writing still hold true for the more experienced job hunter, consideration should be given to the special circumstances discussed below.

Q: When writing my résumé, how far back should I go in listing the positions I've held?

A: Remember that the résumé's purpose is not to provide detailed documentation of all the positions you've ever held. While it may be frustrating to omit past experiences and skills that have played a role in making you the strong candidate you are, you would be better served to carefully select the jobs and responsibilities that are most relevant *to the reader.*

Generally speaking, go back ten years or your last three jobs. Jobs held in the more distant past may be too outdated to be of interest to a potential employer, or might be better discussed in an interview. Use your judgment here. If duties you performed on the job fifteen years ago are a perfect match for those required for the job you want now, note them on your résumé, either in a job description or in a summary of skills.

Q: How long should my résumé be? I have a lot of ground to cover.

A: Strive for brevity, even if that's difficult. If you have more than ten years' experience overall, it is perfectly acceptable to write a two-page résumé. It is almost never acceptable to write a résumé longer than two pages. Remember that prospective employers look at a résumé for only a few seconds and that the second page gets an even briefer glance than the first. Think carefully about the needs of your reader and what she will find relevant, and don't worry excessively about including every skill you have.

Q: I have spent many years gaining experience in one field and now am making a switch to something entirely different. How can I still write a résumé that showcases my strengths?

A: Career changers need to put extra thought into assessing and describing transferable skills. Which of the required skills of the new position do you already possess from some prior experience?

Consider using the functional format for your résumé, and list the broad skill areas at the top of the first page. Then, briefly list a work history toward the bottom of your résumé. Another alternative is to use font size or underlining to highlight the companies you've worked for, listing job titles in smaller print. You may also need to change your cover letter to make mention of your extensive experience, your career change, and your unique qualifications for the new position.

Q: How do I effectively describe the various training sessions or workshops I've participated in?

A: You have a couple alternatives. For one, you could include this information in the "Education" section of your résumé. Using the same format in which you listed attendance at a college or university, note the sites, dates, and titles of the workshops or training sessions you've attended. Or, you could mention these training sessions at the end of the description of each job. For example, after "Supervised 25 customer service representatives," you might add, "Completed training seminars in Effective Management and Creating and Maximizing Work Teams."

Q: How do I account for the years I was unemployed while raising a family, traveling, or attending school?

A: Arrange your résumé so that the reader has a moment to be impressed with your experience before wondering about the gaps in your job history. Don't be untruthful, but list your employment by the years instead of by months and years, and list the dates at the end of a job description or at the bottom of the page. Also, don't neglect to list time spent volunteering, working for yourself, or working as a consultant. Some job hunters mention their travels or unpaid work in their cover letters, but most address these issues during the interview.

Q: I've held many positions within the same company. What's the correct way to include them all in a résumé?

A: Rather than sticking with the convention of listing all employment by date, employer, and title, begin the "Experience" portion of the résumé with the name of the company, displayed in a prominent way. Then indent, listing your job titles and descriptions and dates in reverse chronological order. This technique effectively demonstrates the breadth of experience you've gained at a single workplace and shows that you've moved up in the company.

DIANE L. GRAHAM
3108 Silver Lake Drive
Maitland, Florida 34701
407-229-1182

OBJECTIVE
Management position with company involved in emergency response activities.

EMPLOYMENT

VICE PRESIDENT FOR CORPORATE DEVELOPMENT   1997–PRESENT
TOPP Information, Ltd.   *Maitland, Florida*
Perform consultant duties for all clients, direct emergency outreach and public affairs activities, and facilitate focus groups. Serve as contractor for the U.S. Environmental Protection Agency's (EPA) Emergency Community Outreach Team. Develop and continually update pocket guide for emergency response. Participate as a team trainer for Crisis Communications course. Placed on 24-hour call to man incident command post for national emergency response per federal guidelines.

PUBLIC INFORMATION MANAGER   1988–1997
Rural/Metro, Inc.   *Orlando, Florida*
Served as media spokesperson with responsibility for governmental and public affairs. Managed the advertising and public relations budgets and community service programs, and coordinated internal and external community activities. Served on state-level Emergency Medical Services (EMS) committees while working closely with operations as a member of the Corporate Communications Strategic Planning Team.

PARAMEDIC/SENIOR PARAMEDIC   1986–1988
Rural/Metro, Inc.   *Orlando, Florida*
Emergency patient care and front-line supervision. Served regularly as County Operations Supervisor.

FIREFIGHTER/PARAMEDIC   1989–1990
City of Oviedo   *Oviedo, Florida*
Part-time firefighter/paramedic. Provided emergency patient care.

EDUCATION

BACHELOR OF ARTS   1997
Rollins College   *Winter Park, Florida*
Major: Organizational Communication. Graduated cum laude.

QUALIFICATIONS

- Florida Certified Paramedic
- Incident Command System level 100, 200 and 300—USCG
- Joint Information Center (JIC) training—USCG
- HazWOPER certificate—Hazardous Waste Operations and Emergency Response
- EMS Public Information, Education & Relations Instructor for National Highway Traffic Safety Administration (NHTSA)

HONORS

- The Multiple Public Safety Program Award for 1997—Rural/Metro Corporation
- The 1995 Charles C. Hall Award—Orange County Department of EMS
- The 1988 Internal EMS Week National Award—American Ambulance Association

Sample 6.13: Chronological Résumé for Experienced Worker

Cole Jameson 38 North Bend Drive, Seabrook, SC 87501   878-217-7577

Cjameson@snco.net

Summary

Over 15 years of progressive technical and analytical software systems development experience. Involved with mission-critical projects from conception through analysis, design development, and implementation using structured methodologies. Well-versed with 3-tier client/server architectures and object-oriented technologies.

Technical Summary

Languages: C/C++, Java, VB, PowerBuilder, Perl, SQL, Assembler

Experience

1993–Present   SENIOR SYSTEMS CONSULTANT
Carolinian Financial
Charlotte, SC

Responsibilities: As a senior client/server architect and developer, developed several mission-critical client/server applications as well as infrastructure for use by development projects for field and home office applications, researched object-oriented technologies for line of business application development projects, and mentored application developers.

Designed GUI and developed a mission-critical system providing LAN and dial-up access to multiple legacy systems with an integrated logon security feature to roll and synchronize passwords on multiple tiers. System is being deployed on all field workstations across the country.

Designed and developed API services for client/server applications connected to corporate network via LAN, WAN, and dial-up networking for logon authentication and role-based security, LU 2 host access, automatic dialing, registry access, and other Win32 services.

Designed and developed data distribution for 3-tier client/server sales force automation system in C/C++ for sales and marketing organization. Developed utility to restore referential integrity to customer databases.

Developed 32-bit HLLAPI interface layer between legacy host applications and 600-seat client teleservicing center application implemented in PowerBuilder 6.5. Converted DOS HLLAPI agent commission system written in C and Assembler to run under Windows 95.

Sample 6.14: Chronological Résumé for Experienced Worker

Cole Jameson

Designed and developed a password provider service for single sign on to local workstation, server, and host, saving $300,000 over vendor solution. Disassembled OS to integrate service with the Windows 95 Password Control Panel. Developed thinking layer for 16-bit applications.

Evaluated and recommended software test automation, configuration management, and defect tracking systems for general corporate use. Researched and commended partition table management solution for software testing lab, saving $120,000 in hardware costs.

Researched Java, CORBA, COM+, and other object-oriented component technologies for use in enterprise distributed-computing applications. Recommended move to a thin client architecture for new development.

1983–1993   CONSULTANT
C. R. Jameson Associates
Cambridge, MA

Provided software design, development services, and technical coordination for project that created Ashton-Tate's RapidFile product.

Provided programming services, systems, and support for businesses and organizations.

1989–1991   CONSULTANT
Lotus Development Corporation
Cambridge, MA

Designed database access library for proprietary object-oriented language (LEAF) extending Lotus 1-2-3 releases for DOS & Windows.

Co-developed Lotus Extended Application Facility runtime support.

Automated and enhanced build process.

Education

Eastern College, Dalton, MA
B.A., Chemistry, 1974

Listed in *Who's Who in American Colleges and Universities*. President of Student Outreach Society

References available upon request.

Sample 6.14: Chronological Résumé for Experienced Worker (continued)

WENDY KEELER

83 Woodbine Drive
Howard, NH 74213
(765) 321-1962

SUMMARY OF SKILLS

- *Nine years of experience in service assurance in a five-state district*
- *Experienced corporate troubleshooter*
- *Effective manager of team of 30 employees*
- *Extensive training in leadership, diversity, service assurance, workplace safety*

EMPLOYMENT

FedEx Express Corporation

Service Assurance Manager, *Northeast District Office.*

Improved service and quality within the Northeast District Domestic Ground Operations, which included ME, NH, VT, and portions of NY and MA. Collaborated with a network of agents, operations, and senior management to improve tracking, scanning, and delivering packages on time. Developed and implemented a system of root cause analysis of failed deliveries. Traveled to various hub, metroplex, and ramp facilities to ensure efficient and timely loading and departure of aircraft. Responsible for troubleshooting and designing remediation for any issue affecting service. Compiled, submitted, and presented data to local, regional, and corporate levels for analysis. 1994–2003.

Operations Manager, *Wilmington, MA; Londonderry, NH.*

Supervised team of 15–30 customer-service agents, trailer drivers, couriers, and package handlers on day, night, and weekend shifts. Balanced daily workload of packages to ensure 100% on-time delivery. Monitored hours to meet budgets. Supervised sorts and reload operations. Monitored compliance with all DOT and FedEx road requirements. Investigated incidents and accidents involving FedEx vehicles. Interviewed, hired, and trained all couriers, agents, and handlers. 1987–1994.

Sample 6.15: Chronological Résumé for Experienced Worker

Wendy Keeler

Customer Service Agent, *Londonderry, NH.*
Dispatched calls to drivers, processed packages over the station counter, handled customer complaints, entered payroll, and compiled daily revenue paperwork. 1983–1987.

EDUCATION

B.S., Office Administration, *minors in French and Psychology, Falmouth State College, Falmouth, NH, 1985.*

FedEx training courses*: Service Agent training, International Freight Handling, Dangerous Goods Handling, Defensive Driving, Driver Instructor training, Containerized Vehicle Management Leadership, Safety Management, Diversity, Courier Best Practices, Point-of-Sale Device, Service Assurance. 1984–2003.*

Intensive Leadership Training, *Eckerd College, St. Petersburg, FL, 1988.*

Microsoft Excel, Intermediate Excel, PowerPoint, Access, and various seminars for women in leadership roles, 1994–2002.

AWARDS AND HONORS

Received 33 Bravo Zulu commendation letters for performance above and beyond, 1985–2002.

Lieutenant, Member at Large, Portland Power Squadron, 2002.

FedEx Star Award, 1999.

FedEx Staff Award, 1994.

FedEx Delegate, Maine Quality Forum, 1995.

REFERENCES

Available upon request.

Sample 6.15: Chronological Résumé for Experienced Worker (continued)

Résumé Alternatives

Although chronological and functional résumés are the most common formats for presenting one's experience, they are not the only options. Using an alternative format can help you stand out in a crowd. It can also be seen as a fresh way to organize information that transcends job descriptions and dates of employment.

Sometimes an alternative résumé can be used in conjunction with your traditional résumé. You'll have to decide what is most appropriate for your individual situation. Here are some résumé alternatives to consider:

Narrative résumés. These are conversational in tone, telling a story about the candidate's career progression while integrating relevant personal data. Stick to one page, and break up long blocks of text with headlines and subheads. You may also want to use bullets to present information. The narrative résumé may be combined with a letter starting with a personal greeting, such as "Dear Ms. Smith: I am pleased to send you further information about my work experience, as you requested."

Biographies. In this context, a biography presents a concise, interesting story about your background and most impressive accomplishments. Keep this summary to about five or six paragraphs. Lay out the information on a single page, using an easy-to-read typeface and possibly some graphic elements, like a border or even a head-and-shoulders photo of yourself.

Addenda. An addendum is a single page that accompanies your résumé and describes a particular skill or position in more detail. It gives you the opportunity to elaborate on your most impressive or relevant experience. Good topics for an addendum include: key volunteer, internship or life experiences; computer skills, including hardware, software, and networking systems used; training experiences, including classes taught or attended; and project leadership, including the number of staff, budget, and goals accomplished.

Curriculum vitae. Although occasionally used by people in the medical community, curriculum vitae are most often utilized when applying for work with a firm outside the United States. A curriculum vitae tends to be much more detailed than a traditional résumé—as long as four or five pages. In addition to information about work background and education, it may also note international travel experience and language skills; a listing of references and their contact information; and personal data such as nationality, passport number, birth date, and marital status.

Job-search business cards. If your job hunt is well targeted, the key points of the search will fit on a business card printed on one or both sides, or in a fold-over tent format. These points would include one to three areas of expertise, your job-search goal, and your name and contact information. Distribute your business cards at networking meetings, social events, business open houses, job fairs, and interviews.

Work samples. If you have been previously employed or have taken courses directly related to the job for which you're applying, consider sending actual examples of your work to potential employers. These samples should be truly reflective of the quality of work you do. They should be accompanied by an explanatory cover letter and a traditional résumé. Keep in mind that your work samples may not be returned to you, so you may want to send photocopies.

Résumé Software

You might want to add a résumé software package to your repertoire of job-hunting tools. Although some packages tend to be a bit simplistic and generic in terms of the types of résumés they create, they can certainly serve as a good starting point.

Most packages offer the option of creating either a functional or chronological résumé and provide several templates for each. Depending on the sophistication of the package, you'll have varying degrees of flexibility from there. Some packages offer choices of fonts, graphic elements, colors, and layouts. Many are actually glorified word-processing programs. Just make sure that the package you choose gives clear, step-by-step instructions for inputting information.

Probably the best reason for investing in résumé software is to customize your résumé for different employers. Some software will simplify that task and create crisp, professional layouts as well.

You can purchase résumé software packages at any office-supply or computer store. Packages cost from $20 to $75, depending on their capabilities. Read the boxes carefully, and decide which bells and whistles you really need.

The important thing to remember is that résumé software is not a substitute for your creative thinking and knowledge of the job market. If you rigidly follow the résumé format that came with your computer and its word-processing software, your résumé will look exactly like those of thousands of people who also use that software. To create an effective résumé, you, and only you, must determine how to present your skills and experience in the best light for the type of position you seek. Customize your résumé, and be sure to follow all the basic résumé dos and don'ts. Take extra care that the final layout is pleasing and not too "busy."

Make Your Résumé Computer Friendly

In today's highly automated work environment, many companies turn to computers to store résumés, cover letters, and job applications. Using résumé scanning software and automated applicant tracking systems, companies can easily file and retrieve applicant information. Many companies also use Internet databases to locate applicants. For these reasons, it makes good sense to have a scannable version of your résumé and cover letter. This applies even if you send them only to those employers you know are using automated systems or entering applicant information on the Internet. Following is a list of simple guidelines that will help ensure your data is accurately scanned.

1. **Send originals.** Photocopies or faxed copies often lack clarity and are difficult to scan. If you must send a fax for the purpose of speed, follow up by sending the originals by mail, and mention in your cover sheet that you are doing so.

2. **Choose white or off-white paper.** Text printed on colored paper lacks contrast and can be difficult to read. Very few computers have the ability to read text with low contrast. Use only black ink for the same reason.

3. **Use 8½" by 11" paper, printed on one side.** Many scanners can't handle larger paper sizes. Information printed on a second side may be missed or can make both sides harder for a scanner to read.

4. **Select easy-to-read sans serif fonts.** Avoid fancy type styles. Stick with popular styles such as Helvetica or Arial, in point sizes of 10 to 14. Don't compress any lines of text, and don't print your résumé using a dot-matrix printer or a worn printer cartridge.

5. **Avoid using scripts, italics, underlining, or boldface text.** These features can destroy text clarity, because characters can run together. Although most newer software programs can read these styles, you have no way of knowing what program your recipient uses. Eliminate these features from your résumé by copying the file you used to create your printed version and removing the format commands.

6. **Avoid horizontal and vertical lines.** Any extra lines can be misread. For instance, vertical lines are sometimes read as the letter *I*.

7. **Use wide—at least 1-inch—margins.** Text in the marginal area may be missed.

8. **Avoid graphics.** Any information placed within a graphic can be lost. Steer clear of boxes and shading, as well.

9. **Skip hollow bullets.** If you list information with bullets, use solid dots instead of hollow ones. Computers read hollow dots as the letter *o*.

10. **Use parentheses around the area code in telephone numbers.** Place your area code within parentheses, as opposed to offsetting it from the rest of the telephone number with a hyphen or a slash. Because computers identify phone numbers by searching for parentheses, avoid using parentheses anywhere else in the document.

11. **Separate your e-mail address, phone number, and fax number.** List your e-mail address, phone number, and fax number on different lines, to avoid the chance of a scanner running them together.

12. **No folds, no staples.** Send your letter and résumé in a 9" by 12" envelope, to avoid creases from folding. Use a paper clip to attach the pages, because

staples have to be removed before the pages can be fed into the scanner. Folds and holes impair the scanning software's ability to read the document. Be sure to put your name and a page number at the top of each page, in case the pages separate.

Using Keywords

When résumés and cover letters are scanned or downloaded, the data contained in them are placed in a database for retrieval when a need arises. Employers and recruiters search résumé databases using keywords—nouns and phrases that highlight areas of expertise, industry-related jargon, achievements, and other distinctive features of an applicant's work history.

In wording your résumé for the computer, verbs—the hallmark of a good paper résumé—are less useful than nouns, because recruiters more often search for nouns. You should even be conscious of the form of the nouns you use. *Management,* for example, can be dangerous because it could be missed by a recruiter who typed in *manager.* Your best bet is to include both words. You may even want to have a section, called "Keywords," that unabashedly plays to the computer, seeking to maximize the number of times your résumé pops up in employer searches.

The job seeker with the most keywords, plus the required experience, rises to the top of the candidate heap. Cover your bases by lacing your résumé and cover letter with career-specific keywords.

Which keywords are most effective? This depends on your career objective and the type of position you're hoping to obtain. For example, here is a brief list of keywords that could help land a candidate for a teaching position on an employer's "hit list":

- Private school
- Public school
- Special education
- Master's degree
- Guidance counselor
- Detail oriented
- School board
- Extracurricular activities
- Gifted students
- Inner-city schools
- Teacher-of-the-year award
- Budget planning
- Textbook author

- Computer literate
- Microsoft Office
- Spreadsheet development

EXERCISE   Review your résumé, and make a list of keywords contained in it. Then, look for opportunities to insert additional keywords. Revise your résumé accordingly.

Keywords Used   *New Keywords to Use*

_____   _____

_____   _____

_____   _____

_____   _____

_____   _____

_____   _____

Posting Your Résumé

Now that you've created a scannable version of your résumé, you're ready to post it on the Internet. Different posting sites and services offer varying ways for employers to access résumé databases. Some allow employers, and job candidates too, direct access. Others require that employers tell the service what kind of job they want to fill and what qualifications they seek. The database service then searches the database and provides the employer with résumés from suitable applicants. When deciding whether to post your résumé on a particular site, be sure to determine the answers to the following questions:

- Does the database post the kinds of jobs that interest you?
- Would your ideal employer be likely to search this database?
- How long does a résumé stay in the system?
- What are the posting requirements?
- Are there any costs associated with posting your information?
- Can access to your résumé be restricted in any way, such as to prevent your current employer from being able to see it?

Strategic posting and routine monitoring are your best means of increasing the likelihood of job-hunting success and of ensuring that your résumé doesn't float aimlessly all over the Internet.

Writing Cover Letters

Chapter 7

STRATEGIES in ACTION

Viktor had finally developed a workable résumé. He even had several versions, one for each of the jobs he was going to pursue, all critiqued by professionals in his field. He was proud of himself for negotiating the bureaucracy and getting some very helpful contact names and job titles at several major employers in his area. A good résumé and a solid lead were not enough, however. Viktor needed a cover letter to link the two together.

Viktor reviewed the first draft of his cover letter and made sure it included the three parts of an effective letter: the first paragraph, where he indicated his interest in a specific position; the second paragraph, where he expanded on his education and experience, citing a few specifics; and the final paragraph, where he requested an interview. He was sure this letter would put his résumé—and himself—to work.

Elements of the Cover Letter

When most people think of job hunting, they tend to focus on preparing a résumé. In fact, the cover letter deserves as much, if not more, attention. The cover letter is your chance, in narrative form, to introduce yourself, describe your strengths and skills, and express your interest in a particular job.

More and more, employers look at your cover letter as an indicator of your writing skills. A well-written cover letter can help you stand out from the crowd. It encourages the potential employer to give consideration to your résumé and, ultimately, to interview you for the position.

Because a cover letter is also a way to indicate formal application for a specific position, it can be called a *letter of application* and is usually accompanied by a résumé. A cover letter comprises three main elements:

1. **Introductory paragraph.** The first paragraph mentions the position you're interested in and how you learned of the opening (if indeed you have learned of an opening). If a friend or business contact told you about the position, mention his name, and be sure to send him a copy of your letter. In this paragraph, you may also want to specify why you're applying to this particular company (i.e., because of its outstanding reputation in the field). This paragraph is normally two to four sentences long.

   If you are sending a mass mailing to many companies over a large area, in addition to focusing on the type of position you seek, it would also be advisable to introduce some of your abilities that would be of interest to an employer. If you are sending a cover letter to a specific company and don't know whether there is an opening, begin by explaining the type of position you want and why you are especially interested in working for that company.

2. **Body.** In the middle two paragraphs, "toot your own horn"—honestly of course. In this section, mention at least three of your strong points. One good technique is to use the first paragraph of the body to explain your educational background and the second to describe your work experience. The more specifics you can list, the better. Also, mention personal qualities that suggest you're a highly desirable employee. Are you energetic, enthusiastic, detail oriented, and a fast learner? Choose adjectives that are applicable to the position you want. Use the body of your cover letter to make a connection to the employer.

   If you didn't already mention in your introduction why you want to work for this particular employer, this is the place to do it. Make a crystal-clear correlation between your skills and the needs and character of the company. Your careful research about the company should impress the reader.

3. **Closing.** Don't forget the overall purpose of your cover letter and résumé: to obtain an interview. Be sure to indicate specifically and assertively what you want the employer to do next; for example, "I'd like to arrange an interview at your earliest convenience" is a clear statement. Mention how and where you can be reached, or indicate that you'll call the employer on a specific day. The tone of this section should be polite yet explicit.

The Write Stuff

Keep these tips in mind regarding cover letters:

1. **The best cover letters reveal your enthusiasm for a particular job and the employer, and tell the employer why you are worthy of consideration.** The cover letter is your initial "knock on the door," your chance to make that all-important first impression. In today's highly competitive job market, your cover letter has to be as dynamic and impressive as your résumé . . . and your personality.

2. **Don't send a résumé without a cover letter.** Why pass up an opportunity to present your best qualities? Your cover letter puts your résumé in context, drawing attention to your strengths and best attributes. It gives you a chance to reveal your personality in a way that a strictly formatted résumé does not. At a basic level, it allows you to demonstrate your writing skills. But most importantly, it serves as an introduction to your résumé, a teaser that encourages the reader to take the time to learn more about you.

3. **Personalize your cover letter.** If you address your letter to a specific individual rather than to "Dear Sir," "To Whom It May Concern," or "Human Resources Department," your letter has a much better chance of being read. To get the

name of the appropriate individual, call the company for information, check trade publications and reference materials that list company officers, search the Internet for company information, or find out from a personal contact. Invest your energy in doing solid research so you can aim your cover letter at a target person who makes hiring decisions.

4. **Make sure your letter looks professional.** Type and spell-check your letter. Typos, misspellings, grammatical errors, and cross-outs immediately communicate that you lack written communication skills and don't pay attention to detail. If you are unsure of your writing abilities, ask a professor, coworker, or friend to proofread your work. Even the best writers have editors; enlist several of your own.

5. **Keep your letter to one page.** Your cover letter should be concise but thorough. The length will depend on how much you have to convey, but a total of three to six paragraphs should allow you to cover the most important points. Devote one paragraph to each key thought. Short paragraphs (no more than three or four sentences each) make your letter easy to read.

6. **Familiarize yourself with standard letter formats.** The sample letters in this chapter follow standard rules for spacing and punctuation. Demonstrate your written communication skills by creating professional-looking and -sounding letters. If you are unsure of proper letter format, copy one of the samples in this chapter. Many find the full-block format, as used in the sample letter written to Jennifer Yardley on page 116, the easiest to follow.

7. **Make your cover letter scannable.** Today's cover letters are often read by computers as well as by humans. They are scanned into applicant databases, along with résumés. To ensure proper scanning of your letter, use black type on white or off-white paper. Choose an easy-to-read typeface such as Helvetica or Arial in a point size between 10 and 14. Avoid graphics, bold and italic type, and underlining. Mail your letter and résumé paper-clipped, not stapled, and unfolded in a 9" by 12" envelope.

EXERCISE

A good cover letter takes into account the following questions. Think of the type of position and employer you are seeking, and answer the questions accordingly.

1. Who is the person who will most likely read this letter? What type of person is she? List at least five descriptive phrases. Of course, if you've never met this person, you'll be forced to make some assumptions. The point is that if you're writing a letter to a banker, you should probably phrase your letter more formally than if you were writing a letter to the creative director of an advertising agency.

2. What do you think is important for the reader to know about you?

3. Why will your letter be interesting and important to the reader? What's in it for him?

What Not to Write in Your Cover Letter

Here's a humorous collection of sentences that were found on real cover letters. (They were submitted by various human resource departments.)

- I demand a salary commiserate with my extensive experience.
- Wholly responsible for two (2) failed financial institutions.
- Reason for leaving last job: maturity leave.
- It's best for employers that I not work with people.
- Let's meet, so you can "ooh" and "aah" over my experience.
- You will want me to be Head Honcho in no time.
- Am a perfectionist and rarely if if ever forget details.
- I was working for my mom until she decided to move.
- I have an excellent track record, although I am not a horse.
- I am loyal to my employer at all costs. . . . Please feel free to respond to my résumé on my office voice mail.
- I have become completely paranoid, trusting completely no one and absolutely nothing.
- My goal is to be a meteorologist. But since I possess no training in meteorology, I suppose I should try stock brokerage.
- I procrastinate, especially when the task is unpleasant.
- Instrumental in ruining entire operation for a Midwest chain store.
- Reason for leaving last job: They insisted that all employees get to work by 8:45 A.M. every morning. I couldn't work under those conditions.
- The company made me a scapegoat, just like my three previous employers.

4. What special talents and skills make you a better choice than other applicants?

5. What work experience and educational background do you have that the reader will find significant and relevant?

6. Why would you like to work for the reader's company?

EXERCISE

Once you've written a strong cover letter, you need to decide where to send it. Even if you don't have any definite employer prospects at this point, it would be good practice to begin gathering names. Call local companies in your field and try to obtain the correct name, address, and title of the person you would report to if you were hired in your ideal position. Develop a list of these contacts. Note any difficulties you have eliciting this information, and determine which strategies work best.

Alternative Letter-Writing Strategies

Because no two prospective employers are alike, there's no one way to write cover letters. When seeking an especially competitive position or when stressing unusual skills or abilities, you might consider an alternative to the standard cover-letter format.

Your best bet is to take the information you have about the job opening (from a classified ad, personal contact, library or Internet research, and so on) and use it to craft a letter that fits the needs of the prospective employer. The more you can customize your cover letter, the better. Here are some suggested styles:

Problem/Solution.   Identify the employer's need and describe in your letter how you would be the perfect answer to that need.

Inverted pyramid.   Read the newspaper and you'll see that most news stories are written this way. Put your most important, most relevant information first. Begin with a statement of your career goal and the reasons for your interest in the position, and then move into the specifics of why you're the best candidate.

Deductive order.   Begin your letter with a generalization, almost a thesis statement. Then, support that thesis with examples in the body of the letter. For example, name a specific ability you have. Then, give examples of how you demonstrated that skill in a previous job or at school.

Inductive order.   This is the reverse of deductive order. Begin your letter by describing a specific situation in which you've been involved, and from that example draw the general conclusion that you have a particular skill—one that is necessary for success in the job you're applying for.

List.   Extremely popular, this is one of the most effective formats because of its readability. Insert a bulleted list in the body of your letter. It may be a list of relevant job experiences, related skills, or reasons why you think you're a good candidate for the position.

Types of Cover Letters

Cover letters can be a very effective means of communicating with a potential employer. Seek out opportunities to send them. Because you compose them at your leisure and can therefore give them careful thought, letters often get better results than phone calls.

The three most common types of cover letters are: (1) the letter to generate a lead (also called a *broadcast letter* because it may be sent to many potential employers at the same time); (2) the referral letter (also called a *networking letter*

A résumé should always be accompanied by a cover letter that expresses your enthusiasm for a specific job and clearly states why you are a worthy candidate. (© David Young-Wolff/PhotoEdit)

because it uses one contact to make another); and (3) the response to a classified ad. Here's how to use each type:

Lead-generating letter.   Use this type of letter when you've identified a company you'd like to work for but don't know if any positions are available. You may send out five to ten of these letters or several hundred, depending on the type of job you want and the breadth of your search. The good news is that if you obtain an interview from a lead-generating letter, you'll probably be one of few (or even the only one) being considered for a position. The bad news is that of the many letters you send, only a small percentage, and maybe none at all, will net a response.

Referral letter.   Referral letters often bring excellent results. The mere mention of a mutual contact can get your letter past the secretary to the decision maker. If you are networking effectively, you'll have many opportunities to send out this type of letter.

Response to a classified ad.   The best thing about responding to a classified ad is that you know that a position exists. Unfortunately, a classified ad in a major publication can generate hundreds of responses, so your cover letter had better be good.

Sample Letters

Once you've written one or two cover letters, you'll find it's a cinch to write more. In fact, you'll probably be able to use much of the same wording with minor modifications in future letters.

EXERCISE

Read the sample cover letters on the following pages. They are written in several formats, all equally acceptable. Now it's time to create your own. Compose three cover letters, the first a lead-generating letter, the second a referral letter, and the third a response to a classified ad clipped from a newspaper or trade publication.

This assignment may take some time, but it is a worthwhile endeavor. Although this is a practice exercise, you may still want to use the name, address, and title of a person you wish to contact later in your job search. Show your letter to instructors, employers you know, and friends. Use their feedback to hone your work.

Once you have revised these three letters, you can use them, or modifications of them, in your actual job search. When you've finished this exercise, give yourself a hearty pat on the back. You've just completed one of the most arduous tasks of job hunting—the writing of your first cover letters.

14 Hill Street
Middletown, SD 61604
February 24, 2003

Ms. Jennifer Yardley
Vice President
Technopro, Inc.
672 Charles Avenue
Bedford, SD 61604

Dear Ms. Yardley:

Is your company looking for an experienced, detail-oriented bookkeeper? If so, I would very much like to be considered for the position.

In June, I will receive an associate's degree in business from Middletown College. I have been attending school in the evenings while working days as an assistant bookkeeper at Molly's Chinese Restaurant. That experience has enabled me to gain valuable knowledge in bookkeeping while learning the basics of operating a small business.

I would be interested in arranging an interview at your convenience. If you find you do not have an opening at this time, please feel free to pass my résumé along to your colleagues. Thank you for your consideration. I can be reached at 555-8888.

Sincerely,

Christopher George

Christopher George

Enc.

Sample 7.1: Lead-Generating Letter

Seana Stebbins
3499 West Oak Lane
Clarence, NM 60689
(601) 555-7147
E-mail: sstebbins@prodigy.com

April 4, 2003

Mr. Wallace Reed
Sales Manager
Horace Chemicals, Inc.
111 Orange St.
Clarence, NM 60689

Dear Mr. Reed:

I was the kid on the block with the lemonade stand, the student who won the Brownie camera because I sold the most candy bars, the Girl Scout who went to Disney World for free because I moved the most cookies. Sales has always been my forte.

Now, however, my sales expertise has progressed from cookies and candy to medical technology, specifically pharmaceutical products. I'm writing to see if you might have a need for my skills. Briefly, here's what I would bring to the job:

- 5 years with CapCom Pharmaceuticals as sales representative
- CapCom Salesperson of the Year, 2002, 2003
- Instrumental in the launch of three new pharmaceutical products
- Specialized knowledge of cancer treatments
- M.S. degree in chemistry from Purdue College; B.S. in biology from Notre Dame College

My clients and coworkers would describe me as highly energetic, pleasant to work with, and extremely detail oriented. I would welcome the opportunity to meet with you and discuss how I might fit in as a part of the Horace Chemicals sales team.

Enclosed is my résumé. I will contact you next week to set up an appointment. By the way, I'll bring the lemonade and cookies. Old habits are tough to break.

Sincerely,

Seana Stebbins

Seana Stebbins

Enc: Résumé

Sample 7.2: Lead-Generating Letter

220 Boulder Drive
Manchester, WY 73104
May 10, 2004

Mr. Glenn Severance
Director of Human Resources
Acme Corporation
802 Maple Street
Allston, WY 70011

Dear Mr. Severance:

Janine Hudson of your Marketing Department recently informed me of the opening for an administrative assistant. I believe that my educational background and my experience in business qualify me for the position. Please consider this letter as my formal application.

On May 24, I will graduate from New England University with an associate's degree in Business Administration. I have up-to-date knowledge of the field, having completed courses in everything from marketing to managerial finance. I have maintained a 3.6 cumulative average while financing my education myself by working part- and full-time jobs.

As you will note on the enclosed résumé, I have several years' background in business. As a secretary at Wallace's, Inc., I've experienced the day-to-day operation of a large manufacturing company such as yours. I've also demonstrated my managerial skills by supervising and training other employees at ComputerMart.

I look forward to discussing my capabilities and potential with you. You can reach me by writing to the above address or calling me at (307) 555-4242.

Sincerely,

Langdon Kenney

Langdon Kenney

Enc.
c: J. Hudson

Sample 7.3: Referral Letter, Following Up on a Lead

FRANK NAGLE

6688 Glen Haven Circle, Orley Park, VA 44989, (505) 555-3338
Nagle99@mediaone.com

January 6, 2003

Mr. John Zofchack, Vice President
Manley Accounting Services
2220 Conway Ave.
Charleston, VA 44999

RE: Your controller position (referred by Marisol Playa)

Dear Mr. Zofchack:

As an accountant with more than five years in the field, I was excited to learn of your need for an experienced controller. Marisol Playa, a former colleague, suggested I contact you. She thought my experience closely matched your job requirements.

Your needs:	My qualifications:
• Four-year degree	• BS in accounting
• CPA credential	• CPA plus additional course work in financial management
• Experience in report generation	• Compiled data for quarterly and annual reports.
• Accounting software proficiency	• Experience with Excel, Peachtree, Lotus, and various financial analysis programs
• Five years' experience with major accounting firm	• Two years with Whitney Marcel Ltd. as an accountant; three years with Kosmos Corp. as senior accountant/controller

This abbreviated list represents only some of my relevant experience, so I am enclosing my résumé. I am currently employed with Kosmos Corp. but am seeking new and exciting challenges. I will contact you next week in hopes that we can further discuss the requirements of the position. Thank you for your interest.

Sincerely yours,

Frank Nagle

Frank Nagle

Enclosure: Résumé

Sample 7.4: Referral Letter, Following Up on a Lead

Kimba Bartlett
127 D.W. Highway
Kensington, IL 34333
(405) 555-6784
e-mail: kbartlett@aol.com

June 1, 2003

Mr. Kyle Cooke
Office Manager
Midtown Software, Inc.
575 Island Rd.
Kensington, IL 34333

Dear Mr. Cooke:

I am writing to apply for the position of Administrative Assistant as advertised in the *Kensington Ledger* on May 25, 2003.

For the past year I have worked as a secretary at Royer's Hospital in downtown Kensington. My responsibilities are diverse and include receptionist duties, bookkeeping, word processing, and file management.

At the end of this month, I will graduate from Kensington Community College with an associate's degree in liberal arts. I would like to use the skills I've acquired at Royer's combined with my degree from Kensington in an interesting, challenging position.

Enclosed is my résumé. It details the skills I could bring to Midtown Software in the position of administrative assistant. I will contact you next week to discuss how we can explore this possibility further. Thank you for your consideration.

Sincerely,

Kimba Bartlett

Kimba Bartlett

Enclosure: Résumé

Sample 7.5: Response to Classified Ad

1654 Daige Street
Burbank, CA 99877
March 24, 2003

Box J-97
Burbank Times
Opportunity Plaza
Burbank, CA 99877

Re: Collections Agent Position

Please consider me for the position of collections agent as advertised in the March 20 edition
of the *Burbank Times*.

In the past three years, I have had much experience in collections. Frequently, in my position
as a customer service representative at Village Bank, I assisted collections clerks with their
telephone and written inquiries as well as answered many customer questions regarding past-
due accounts. My employers have often complimented me on my attention to detail and my
perseverance in solving difficult problems.

I would appreciate the opportunity to further discuss this position and my qualifications.
Please contact me for an interview at the above address or at (203) 555-2222.

Sincerely,

Shannon Bourke

Shannon Bourke

Enc.

Sample 7.6: Response to Classified Ad

6 Cumberland Ave
Boseman, MD 10365
(312) 874-9065
hdranton@attbi.com

July 17, 2004

Principal Donald O'Neil
Westbrook High School
7568 Mammoth Road
Westbrook, MD 10357

Dear Mr. O'Neil:

I am applying for a full-time position as a science teacher at Westbrook High School beginning September 2004. Having the opportunity to join the quality team of educators at Westbrook High would be a welcome experience.

Enclosed is my résumé for your review. I have completed a bachelor's degree in secondary education at Boseman College and am currently pursuing a master's degree from Olivian University in Lee, Delaware. By the completion of the summer semester, I will have earned 36 of the required 62 credits.

During my student teaching at George Washington Middle School, I collaborated with the science faculty and administrators to develop an earth science curriculum targeting at-risk children in the district. I was able to implement and instruct the first three units of the curriculum, including field trips to study coastal ecosystems. My students and co-teachers especially enjoyed an online dialogue with middle school students studying similar coastal ecosystems in a small town in southern California.

This experience, as well as my work on community projects and with the Girl Scouts of America, demonstrates my commitment to teamwork, my passion for education, and my innovation in the classroom.

My résumé is a brief overview of my professional abilities, but meeting you in an interview would enable me to provide a clearer picture of the type of person I am. Thank you in advance for your time and consideration.

Sincerely,

Holly Antonnucci

Holly Antonnucci
Enc.

Sample 7.7: Lead-Generating Letter

Thomas R. Moser
93 S. Maple Ave
Montgomery, AL 20534
(256) 223-6768

Ms. Caroline DeNauw
New Day Dynamics Associates
99 Farbush St.
Hastings, AL 02534

Dear Ms. DeNauw:

I have learned from our mutual friend, Tyler Phillipian, that you may have a need for an additional counselor at New Day Dynamics Associates. I would very much welcome the opportunity to be considered for the position, in which I could implement my relevant skills as a member of your practice.

My credentials include:

M.Ed., Agency and Rehabilitative Counseling, Roget College

Certified Alcohol and Drug Rehabilitation Counselor

Seven years' experience, counselor at Greater Montgomery Mental Health

Extensive counseling experience with multicultural and socioeconomically diverse clients

Program and seminar development experience

Member, Committee for Ethical Review, Alabama Mental Health Professional Association

I would greatly appreciate the chance to learn more about the needs of your practice and to explore how my qualifications might meet those needs. I will call early next week to discuss the possibility of an interview.

Sincerely,

Thomas R. Moser

Thomas R. Moser
Enc.
c: T. Phillipian

Sample 7.8: Referral Letter, Following Up on a Lead

Obtaining References and Assembling a Portfolio

Chapter 8

STRATEGIES in ACTION

Lindsay placed a call to her supervisor at her last job. Even though she'd been a server at a local restaurant and was now applying for an administrative position at a doctor's office, she thought the supervisor could testify to her good attitude, work ethic, and people skills. After the initial hellos, Lindsay explained the reason for her call:

Lindsay: April, I'm applying for an administrative position at several medical offices in the area, and I'd like to know if I may use you as a work reference.

April: Sure, Lindsay. I'd be glad to serve as a reference for you. You were always one of my best servers.

Lindsay: I'd appreciate it if you could emphasize how dependable I was and how I always made sure my customers were pleased. I want my prospective employers to know they can rely on me, and that I'll always be professional in dealing with patients.

April: No problem, Lindsay. I can tell the employers who contact me that you had an excellent attendance record and were always on time. I'll explain how we had many regular customers who kept coming back because of your good service. I'll also mention that you were chosen as employee-of-the-month many times.

Lindsay: Thanks, April. That's exactly the kind of information I was hoping you'd pass along. I'll let you know if I get hired. I really appreciate your help.

Lindsay did an excellent job preparing April to serve as her reference. First, she asked April's permission before giving out her name, a nice courtesy. Second, Lindsay told April the type of job she was seeking and mentioned the skills that would be important in such a position. Third, Lindsay promised to let April know if she gets hired—another nice courtesy.

Now Lindsay can be assured April will give her an excellent recommendation and tell prospective employers about specific qualities of her work that would be relevant to the type of position she is seeking.

References Available upon Request

You have a winning résumé and a dynamic cover letter. Now the finishing touch is to line up some stellar references. There are two routes to go here. One is to generate a list of names for the employer to call. Some employers will make the effort to follow up; some don't. The other is to provide the employer with positive letters of recommendation written in advance by your references. These letters can be your ultimate sales tool in getting an employer to choose you.

Whether you opt to take one route or both, the important thing is that you not wait until you're on the verge of getting a job offer before you take care of this important step.

Phone References

Today's employers want to be as confident as possible in their hiring decisions—it's just too costly and time consuming to hire and train the wrong individual. One of the ways employers try to back up the impressions they form of you during an interview is to contact, usually by phone, a few references whose names you provide. These references are people not related to you who can give informed assessments of your job performance and character.

Because glowing references can set you apart from other candidates, it's important to choose your people carefully. To generate your list of phone references, follow these steps:

1. **Make a list of people whom you think might serve as your references.** Former bosses, coworkers, teachers, and guidance counselors are all possible candidates.

2. **Contact the people on your list.** Ask them if they would be willing to be your references. Remind them of the work you did with them and mention things you would like them to tell prospective employers about you. Make sure the individual is comfortable providing a strong reference. If you sense any hesitation, you may want to cross that person off your list. You want only enthusiastic recommendations.

3. **Tell your references about the jobs you're seeking.** This will help your references sound prepared when they're called and enable them to provide the most relevant information to the employer regarding your experience and qualifications.

4. **Keep in touch with your references.** Reconnect with your references every few months to be sure your contact information is up-to-date. Let them know, either by phone, letter, or e-mail, that you're still job-hunting and you appreciate being able to keep them on your reference list.

5. **Be selective in giving your references' names to employers.** You don't want your references barraged by too many phone calls; this could be seen as an annoyance and also might make your references wonder why you're having such a hard time getting a job. If a prospective employer asks for your references before you've even had a face-to-face meeting, explain that your references are very important to you and should be called only if the employer is relatively serious about hiring you.

6. **Ask your references to let you know when they've been called.** This will help you keep tabs on the hiring process. A call to a reference usually suggests that you're a leading candidate for the job. Conversely, if you've given out four names and none has been called within approximately a two-week period, then you're probably not as strong a contender as you might have thought.

7. **Thank your references.** When you are successful in getting a job, it's important to thank your references for their willingness to help and to let them know about your new position, whether or not they played a part. Showing your appreciation is not only the right thing to do; it also makes it easier to ask them again to serve as a reference should the need arise.

Letters of Recommendation

In addition to or instead of phone references, you may want to consider providing a prospective employer with letters of recommendation. The strongest references come from previous employers who can vouch for your knowledge, integrity, and enthusiasm toward work. Your best bet is to get a reference from an immediate supervisor, manager, or coworker. The higher the professional status, the better, although the reference writer must be familiar with who you are and what you did. If you think it would be helpful, you may even want to get references from several people at the company.

Keep in mind that you don't have to have been a full-time employee to get a letter of recommendation; requesting references at places where you were employed part-time, interned, volunteered, or freelanced is entirely appropriate. Ideally, you should begin gathering letters of recommendation either just before you leave a position or soon afterward, while the quality of your work is still fresh in the mind of the letter writer. As with phone references, request letters only of people who think positively of you. If you believe that your manager is unlikely to give you a good reference, consider asking your immediate supervisor or even a coworker.

Other potential letter writers may include teachers, guidance counselors, leaders of organizations or clubs, or other people familiar with your work. They should all be professional contacts. Personal references from friends, neighbors, or relatives should be used rarely, and then only in cases where the employer needs a character reference, such as for positions in child care or law enforcement.

How Do You Get a Letter of Recommendation?

The easiest way to get a letter of recommendation is to ask your supervisor or manager. Tell that person about the type of position you're seeking so the letter can be focused toward your objective. Also, give the writer a deadline—politely, of course—to ensure that your letter is treated as a priority.

Whereas some people are quite adept at letter writing, some may find the task challenging or may be so busy they can't comply within your time frame. You can help speed the process along and ensure the content of the letter by following these steps:

1. **Prepare a draft of your letter of recommendation.** You'll learn in the next section exactly what that letter should include.

2. **Hand deliver or mail to your reference person both a disk and a printed copy of your recommendation letter.** Another option is to send your draft by e-mail. No matter how you choose to submit your materials, be sure to include a cover letter inviting your reference to review your draft, edit it, and return the final draft signed and on company letterhead.

3. **After receiving your letter of recommendation, make copies of it.** Don't send an original to a prospective employer; you may not get it back.

4. **Send a thank-you note to the person who wrote your letter.** A note will help ensure a positive referral should the individual be personally contacted by a potential employer seeking additional information.

What Should a Letter of Recommendation Say?

If you are drafting your own letter, be sure to do the following:

1. Identify your reference—her position and how she knows you.

2. State who is being recommended (namely you), and for what type of position.

3. Describe the reference's relationship to you—how long you worked together, in what capacity, and specific projects that you worked on together.

4. List your top skills, qualities, work habits, attributes, and achievements.

5. Mention that the reference can be contacted for additional information.

6. If your reference person prefers to write his own letter, verbally review the above points with him, to ensure the effectiveness of the letter. A letter of recommendation lacking these points of information won't help your case.

How Many Recommendations Are Enough?

Six references should be the maximum, but even one or two can help sway a prospective employer. Rather than quantity, focus on quality. Be sure the letters present you in the best light and are consistent with how you describe yourself in your résumé and during interviews.

When Should You Submit Your Letters of Recommendation?

There is no hard-and-fast rule about when to give a prospective employer your letters of recommendation. Because they are not routinely requested in the way that a résumé or job application is, you'll have to use your judgment. If your letters are relevant to the job you're applying for and are extremely positive, you may want to include them with your résumé and cover letter. If you think your résumé and cover letter are strong enough to stand on their own, wait until the interview or until they're requested to present them. Treat your letters as another tool of persuasion in convincing the prospective employer you are the best candidate for the job.

CARLA MORAN

5585 Kensington Way
Brooklyn, NY 98921
(404) 555-7534
Carmor@bny.com

April 12, 2003

Mr. Kevin Lorita
Vice President, Human Resources
Sundown Corporation
338 Orleans Lane
Brooklyn, NY 98921

Dear Kevin:

As you know, I will be graduating in June and am seeking full-time employment as a human resources representative back in my hometown of Charlotte, South Carolina. I would greatly appreciate it if you could write a letter of recommendation for me regarding my work in your department as a human resources coordinator during the last two years.

I have taken the liberty of drafting a letter to help expedite the process. Feel free to edit the letter or write one of your own. Then please return the final draft to me on company letter-head by April 24, 2003, if at all possible.

Thank you in advance. I will say in touch and keep you apprised of my job search.

Sincerely,

Carla Moran

Carla Moran

Enclosure

Sample 8.1: Cover Letter to Request a Letter of Recommendation

Sundown Corporation
338 Orleans Lane
Brooklyn, NY 98921
(404) 555-1121

April 20, 2003

To Whom It May Concern:

Carla Moran worked as a human resources coordinator for two years in my department at Sundown Corporation. During that time, Carla had diverse responsibilities. She reviewed résumés to identify qualified employment candidates, conducted preliminary applicant interviews, and documented hiring-firing policy, decisions for distribution to Sundown's various department supervisors.

Carla is bright, articulate, and hard working. Her enthusiasm for the job comes through in all she does. She has a positive attitude that makes her a pleasure to work with and is one of the reasons she was so well liked by her coworkers.

I highly recommend Carla for any job she is considering in the human resources field. She would be an asset to any employer. If you have further questions about Carla, please do not hesitate to contact me at (404) 555-1121, ext. 200.

Sincerely,

Kevin Lorita

Kevin Lorita
Vice President, Human Resources

Sample 8.2: Letter of Recommendation Proposed by the Job Hunter

Assemble a Portfolio

Although artists and architects have traditionally used portfolios as part of their job application process, professionals in other fields have only begun to see their value as a means of differentiating themselves from other applicants. Think of a portfolio as another opportunity to present evidence of your skills and build your case as the best candidate for the job.

What Should a Portfolio Contain?

The first two elements can be a list of phone references followed by letters of recommendation, both mentioned earlier in this chapter. Although the contents of your individual portfolio will, of course, depend on your field and the type of position you're seeking, some other items to consider including are:

Licenses.   Include photocopies of any professional certifications related to your field, demonstrating that you have met the requirements and passed the necessary skills tests for work in a specific area.

Letters of commendation.   Like letters of recommendation, these statements from credible sources serve as third-party endorsements, testifying to your skills and accomplishments.

Awards.   Include documentation of any awards or special recognition you've received that relate to your profession.

Work samples.   Showcase any items of your work that demonstrate your capabilities. These can be reports, project write-ups, examples of your writing, PowerPoint presentations, computer programs, drawings, photographs, manuals, blueprints, business plans, and so on. If you are a recent graduate, these work samples may have been generated in courses you took. As you gather experience in your career, however, you'll want to replace schoolwork with professional work.

Performance reviews.   Excellent reviews from previous employers demonstrate your work ethic and skills. If you're a recent graduate, you can include copies of your transcripts, highlighting in particular those courses related to your field.

Certificates.   If you've completed certain courses or attended a professional conference or workshop, you may have received certificates of completion. These certificates demonstrate that your skills are current and that you are committed to professional growth.

Publicity.   Perhaps you've received some publicity for your work, such as through articles you've published in trade journals or mention you've received in press releases. If so, include copies of this media attention in your portfolio. Be sure to highlight the places where you are mentioned so that the reader can skip right to the relevant material.

Consider assembling a portfolio. It allows you to present samples of your work and additional evidence that you are the best candidate for the job.
(© David Barber/PhotoEdit)

Business cards.   You may want to create a professional business card to leave behind with your interviewers. A business card would include your name, a brief tagline under your name where you'd otherwise see a job title (e.g., "corporate trainer with Fortune 500 experience"), your contact information, and on the back four to five bullet points summarizing your skills or professional accomplishments.

Should Every Employer See Every Component of Your Portfolio?

No. Customize your portfolio before each interview. Include only material that is pertinent to the job you're applying for. It's not quantity that will impress the employer, but rather the substance and relevance of the items.

How Do You Present Your Portfolio?

You can present your portfolio in a binder, a folder, a file, or a portfolio case (available in most office-supply and art-supply stores). Choose a method of display that is professional plus easy to carry and maneuver through.

Consider bringing copies of key items to leave behind for further review if the interviewer should display a keen interest. Never offer your originals, because—despite the interviewer's best intentions—there's no way to guarantee when, or even if, they'll be returned.

When Do You Present Your Portfolio?

Because your appointment with an interviewer may be brief or limited to a specifi- cally allotted amount of time, it's a good idea to mention early in the meeting that you've brought along some important credentials to share with her. This allows the interviewer to plan accordingly.

Most likely, the early part of your meeting will be about the job opening, the company, and your career goals. As the discussion moves into areas related specif- ically to your experience and capabilities, look for an opportunity to present your portfolio. Be prepared to narrate the presentation. Keep your comments brief, however, so the interviewer can read and review each item.

One more tip: Watch the interviewer carefully as you present your portfolio materials. Linger on those items that appear to pique his interest, and skim quickly through those that don't. Observe body language to better gauge the in- terviewer's impression of your materials. For example, does he pull your portfolio closer for better scrutiny, or does he swiftly turn pages for a cursory, perhaps somewhat disinterested, quick scan?

Can You Put Your Portfolio Online?

Yes. If you've created a web site to market yourself, many elements of your portfolio will be appropriate for inclusion. You may even be able to e-mail your portfolio to interested employers. Keep in mind, however, that although an electronic portfolio can be a valuable marketing tool, it's no substitute for an in-person interview in which you can narrate its elements, demonstrate your communication skills, and dazzle the employer with your dynamic personality.

Part Three

BEGINNING THE SEARCH

Organizing and Surviving the Job Hunt

Chapter 9

STRATEGIES in ACTION

Unemployed but not discouraged, Haley, a recent college graduate, decided it was time to establish a plan of action for her future. She began by writing a list of daily goals she wanted to achieve. The first item on the list was exercising and establishing a healthy eating routine. She readily admitted that she'd gained the "college 15" while in school and was unhappy with her appearance.

Next on her list was spending a minimum of two hours each day doing specific tasks that would help her find employment. Whether it was researching com-panies, networking, or drafting cover letters to employers, she committed to putting in daily effort toward achieving her goal.

The last major item on her list was continuing her professional development. She would expand her knowl-edge of her field by using a portion of every day to read relevant trade journals and books or search the Internet.

If she stuck with her plan, Haley knew, it wouldn't be long before she lost weight, found employment, and confidently entered her field with a solid knowl-edge base.

Take Care of Yourself

Aside from searching for a job that's right for you, there's something else you should take care of—yourself! A job search takes time. People seeking entry-level or generalized positions can expect their search to take two to four months; those seeking higher-paying or more specialized jobs can expect a search period of six months, a year, or more. Of course, factors such as the state of the economy and the employment situation in your field and locale affect the length of your search as well.

How does one survive such a long and potentially stressful period of time? Concentrate on the five pieces of advice presented in the next sections.

Think of Job Hunting as Your Job

Don't consider this time to be a vacation, and don't let anyone else think of your job search that way, either. Get up early, get dressed, and go to a spot where you can plan your day. Stake out an area to use as your office, and have all your job-search materials readily available. Even if you can't convert a spare bedroom or alcove into an office, assemble in one spot your résumés, stationery, computer, stamps, lists and organizational charts, and most importantly, a phone. An answering machine would be a worthwhile investment.

Whatever you do, don't sleep until noon and lounge around in a sweatsuit snacking on munchies. This mentality is only counterproductive. If you need to take a long weekend for a vacation, do it. Then resume your search.

Be wary of requests to run errands, baby-sit, or do other chores "because you have free time." Establish in your own mind and in the minds of others that, for now at least, finding the right job is your primary occupation.

Practice Time Management and Self-Discipline

Make a "do list" each day and prioritize each item with an A (most important), B (important), or C (least important). When possible, group job-hunting errands. For example, when you go downtown to do research at the library, you could also plan to drop by the post office to buy stamps or mail letters. Build rewards into your day, too, such as meeting a friend for lunch after you've accomplished all your morning tasks.

Take pleasure in checking items off your list, and consider keeping all your lists together in one notebook or folder. Sometimes old lists can remind you of your accomplishments or give you new energy and direction. At the end or beginning of each day, evaluate the items left undone. Place those items on a new list, or reassess and abandon them altogether. Time-management habits such as these are essential to most occupations, and developing them now will be useful not only in your job hunt but also once you're employed.

Get organized and stay focused. Dedicate time each day to specific job-hunting tasks. A sense of accomplishment will help you remain optimistic until your efforts begin to pay off. (© Lon C. Diehl/ PhotoEdit)

Examine the sample list that follows to see how one job hunter organized and prioritized tasks:

SAMPLE JOB HUNTER'S DO LIST

Date: 10/27/02

Check When Completed	Priority	Task
❑	B	Dig up more leads using newspapers at the library.
❑	A	Make follow-up phone calls to J. Curaci at XYZ Corp.
❑	A	Revise résumé objective to fit ad in the *Daily News*.
❑	A	Write thank-you letter to Mr. Lee at Lee's Widgets.
❑	B	Write cover letter for lead given by Uncle Joe.
❑	A	Write thank-you letter to Uncle Joe.
❑	C	Buy more matching envelopes at office supplies store.
❑	B	Call Barton's to find name of contact person.
❑	C	Stop by chamber of commerce for brochures or leads about local industry.

You could also take the next step and plan the order of your day, as shown here:

TIME PLANNER

A.M.	Goals
9:00–10:00	Make phone calls for leads, follow-up, etc.
10:00–11:30	Write letters; revise résumé.
11:30–12:00	Read annual reports and brochures picked up yesterday.

P.M.	
12:00–1:00	Meet Jane for lunch.
1:00–3:30	Research at library.
3:30–4:30	Stop by post office, chamber of commerce, office supplies store.
5:00–6:00	Attend Business After Hours meeting.

Forms to assist you in managing your time are provided on pages 141 and 142.

Set Goals

Keep your purpose in mind, and work toward it to stay productive. Write down your goals and review them periodically. Your daily goal might be to make two new contacts. A weekly goal might be to mail out twenty résumés and cover letters. Whatever the goal, make it specific and measurable, and set a deadline for accomplishing it.

Get Past the Shame Barrier

Your jobless state is not a reflection of your character. It's okay to acknowledge that not having a job is an uncomfortable, and sometimes embarrassing, position to be in. Realize that it's not terminal, however, and that it happens to almost all of us at one time or another. Don't waste time wallowing in depression; set up a plan that helps you take action.

Finally, recognize that your next job may not be your dream job. Employment depends on a variety of factors, only some of which you can control. At the very worst, you'll work in a less-than-ideal position for a little while. At best, you'll find something that's related to your career choice.

Find Outlets for Stress

Do everything you can to keep yourself healthy and calm. Exercise is a great way to clear your head and relieve tension; relaxation techniques can also be helpful. Build a network of supportive friends and family members. If the pressure becomes too intense, see a counselor or visit your rabbi or pastor. To the extent possible, avoid people who discourage you or distract you from the goals you've set. Taking care of your mental and physical health gives you an edge in the job search.

(Photocopy for future use.)

JOB HUNTER'S DO LIST

Date: _____

Check When Completed	Priority (A/B/C)	Tasks
❑	_____	1. _____
❑	_____	2. _____
❑	_____	3. _____
❑	_____	4. _____
❑	_____	5. _____
❑	_____	6. _____
❑	_____	7. _____
❑	_____	8. _____
❑	_____	9. _____
❑	_____	10. _____

Goals

By today's end: _____

_____

By one week from today: _____

_____

Within one month: _____

_____

Within six months: _____

_____

Within one year: _____

_____

(Photocopy for future use.)

JOB HUNTER'S TIME PLANNER

Date: _____

A.M.	Tasks
8:00	_____
8:30	_____
9:00	_____
9:30	_____
10:00	_____
10:30	_____
11:00	_____
11:30	_____

P.M.	
12:00	_____
12:30	_____
1:00	_____
1:30	_____
2:00	_____
2:30	_____
3:00	_____
3:30	_____
4:00	_____
4:30	_____
5:00	_____
5:30	_____
6:00	_____
6:30	_____

Troubleshooting for Job Hunters

If after implementing all the job-hunting techniques mentioned in this guide-book, you find you're still struggling in one or two particular areas, try some of these tips to help you over the trouble spots.

Having Trouble . . . ?	*Try to . . .*
Identifying the type of job you desire	• Interview or job-shadow professionals in various fields. • Peruse the Sunday classified ads in a major newspaper. • Do further reading on jobs. Especially helpful is *The Occupational Outlook Handbook,* a government publication available in most libraries. • Visit career web sites on the Internet.
Getting motivated	• Join a job seeker support group. • Ask a friend or relative to dedicate one hour to helping you write your résumé or cover letter. • Make out a do list. Assign deadlines for each task. Turn off the TV, the stereo, or any other distraction, and force yourself to complete a job-hunting task. • Break a task that is becoming a hurdle into smaller, easy-to-handle parts. Then, focus on completing one part at a time.
Identifying strengths	• Brainstorm a list. • Examine, in writing, areas of your past success. • Ask a friend, family member, or teacher.
Preparing a résumé	• Work on only one section at a time. • Show drafts to people whose opinions you trust. • Experiment with new formats. • Use the Internet to find posted résumés of other people in your field. Adapt some of their ideas to yours.
Generating leads	• Read local newspapers and note active companies. • Find new ways to network. • Join professional associations in your field. • Use the Internet to identify potential employers.

Researching employers	• Use the Internet.
	• Check the library.
	• Visit chambers of commerce.
Using the Internet	• Enlist the help of an Internet-savvy friend or teacher.
	• Begin by visiting some of the general career web sites.
Getting past the personnel office	• Call or visit your potential supervisor directly, especially early or late in the day, when his assistant is not likely to be around.
	• Send an e-mail directly to the individual making the hiring decision.
Networking	• Persistence is the key. Join organizations in your field.
	• Use networking groups.
	• Talk to everyone about your situation.
	• Join an online discussion group related to your career field.
Writing cover letters	• Write out of order. Start with any paragraph you feel comfortable with; eventually the letter will begin to flow. Then, go back and organize the order.
	• Read your drafts from last sentence to first to make sure each sentence alone makes sense.
	• Ask yourself if the letter clearly states what you want and what you have to offer.
	• Allow drafts to sit for a day between revisions.
	• Ask a friend to edit and proofread your draft.
Preparing for interviews	• Practice in a mirror or with friends.
	• Ask and answer questions using a tape recorder.
	• Go to a job fair to get comfortable talking with recruiters.
	• Accept all interviews offered, even if they are not for a position you want, just to get more practice.
	• Write notes on wall or desk calendars.
Keeping track of contacts and progress	• Use do lists; prioritize items on your list.
	• Set aside a special time each day for record keeping.
	• Organize your job search using a filing system.
	• Ask fellow job hunters about their organization systems.

Overcoming shyness	• Say an extra few words to everyone you meet, including cashiers, coworkers, and bank tellers.
	• Consider the possibility that shyness means you're thinking only about yourself. Try to focus on other people and their personalities.
	• Join networking or professional groups and set a goal of meeting at least three new people at each meeting.

Finally, remember that smart people realize when they need extra help. Most community mental health centers offer the services of professional career counselors, and fees are often based on a sliding scale. Colleges have career counselors on staff, and the costs are included in your tuition. Career counselors can also be found on the Internet. They can administer skills or personality inventories, review your résumé, or help you practice interviewing. Take advantage of all the help available to you!

Taking Your Job Hunt Online

Learning Objectives

In this chapter, you'll learn about the Internet and various means of utilizing it in your job hunt to:

- Do industry research
- Do company research
- Search job openings databases
- Post your résumé online
- Participate in online career discussion groups
- Search electronic bulletin boards
- Search newspaper classified ads around the country
- Create your own web page
- Use e-mail
- Locate career products or services
- Conduct salary research
- Learn about a geographic area
- Search major career sites

Chapter 10

STRATEGIES in ACTION

After nearly fifteen years as a stay-at-home mom, Kristina was ready to reenter the work force. In the past, she'd obtained her jobs by the traditional method of responding to classified ads with a résumé and cover letter. But Kristina knew that times had changed and that to do a comprehensive job search she would need to utilize the resources of the Internet.

She began by visiting some of the major career sites she'd heard about from friends. What a wealth of information they held! In addition to job listings, there were wonderful articles on subjects such as résumé writing

and interviewing, online discussion groups where she could chat with other job hunters, bulletin boards where she could post questions and get advice from other job hunters, and locations where she could post her résumé and prospective employers would be likely to see it.

Kristina was surprised at how easy it was to navigate the sites, and she quickly got up to speed in utilizing their many services. Although she still planned to use traditional job-hunting methods such as classified ads and networking, she also realized that the Internet would be a fantastic asset in her search.

Pounding the Virtual Pavement

The New Medium for Job Seekers

Although reading classified ads, cold calling, letter writing, and networking have traditionally been the most widely used means of finding a job, the Internet has emerged as one of the most important tools in the job-search process. With its extensive, easily accessible information, its powerful searching capabilities, and its instant channels of communication, it has revolutionized the way people look for jobs and the way companies recruit.

What Is the Internet?

The Internet is a vast system of millions of interconnected computer networks. This network links individuals, businesses, universities, libraries, and governments throughout the world. Unlike virtually any other medium, no one owns or operates it—it's just there. Although the Internet was a government initiative started in the 1960s, its boom in commercial and educational markets in the past decade or so has sparked new ways of doing business and communicating globally.

The World Wide Web is the fastest-growing part of the Internet. Using a Web browser, people can view information from web sites that other companies or individuals have created. A formatting language, HTML (hypertext markup language), is used to create web pages and establish hypertext links to other web sites. Most Web browsers allow users to view text, graphics, video, and animation on the Web as well as to hear audio. It is also possible to download software programs, conduct online discussions, and purchase items.

Using the Internet to Job-Hunt

The Internet can provide great tools to assist in your job search. You can network; exchange correspondence; gather research on careers, trends, industries, and individual companies; search for job openings; post your résumé; get career advice from professional counselors; and exchange ideas with other job hunters. The Internet is used by many prominent companies to list job openings, accept employee applications, and even conduct interviews online. In fact, the Internet has been called the future of recruiting.

It's Fast; It's Convenient

One of the best characteristics of the Internet is its convenience. You can go online at any time; it's "open" twenty-four hours a day. Doing your research or networking in the evening or on weekends is no problem. Unlike a library or business, the Internet is there whenever you need it.

You should keep in mind, however, that not all information on the Internet is accurate, current, or necessarily true. Be sure to evaluate carefully the quality of Internet data before using it to make an important decision.

Also, the Internet is not a replacement for other types of research and job-hunting tools. Printed materials such as magazines, newspapers, books, and directories are still vital to a comprehensive job search.

Show Employers You Know Your Way around the Internet

Although your level of success on the Internet depends in part on the kind of job you're seeking and how skilled you are in online computing, use of the Internet should still be a major component of your job search. Beyond providing listings of specific job openings, it is an invaluable research tool.

At the very least, job seekers who conduct a cybersearch demonstrate to employers a basic knowledge of personal computers and the Internet. In today's intensely competitive job market, every little advantage counts.

Accessing the Internet

If you don't have a computer, don't despair. Many public libraries and schools offer Internet access through their computers. Take advantage of free resources if you are currently unable to invest in your own computer equipment.

If you do have your own computer and are a student, you can most likely get online free of charge through your school. Visit your school's computer center to obtain any necessary software and to learn what requirements you must meet.

If you are not a student, to get online you'll need a personal computer, an Internet service provider, and a browser to view the World Wide Web. You can use a

The Internet is an excellent resource for information about industries, companies, and even job openings.
(© Spencer Grant/Photo Researchers, Inc.)

service provider that offers the Internet and e-mail only, or an online service that provides Internet access as well as many other online features such as America Online. Service charges vary according to many factors, but they typically range from $15 to $25 a month for unlimited use.

Boosting Your Job Search

You can use the Internet to enhance your job search in many ways, as explained in this section.

Industry research.   Begin by checking trade periodicals. Most publications have their own web sites that highlight key stories relevant to the industry. Next, find the industry's main web sites by checking major search engines like Yahoo! at **www.yahoo.com,** and Excite at **www.excite.com.** Finally, look for discussion groups in the chosen industry. These groups often produce discussion lists about industry-related information and keep articles from back issues of trade periodicals at their web sites.

Company research.   If you have identified a specific company as your desired potential employer, you'll want to know everything you can about it, to better target your cover letter and appear knowledgeable in an interview. Begin by finding the company's web site. Try doing a search using the company's name followed by **.com.** If that doesn't bring up the site you seek, try a keyword search using a major search engine. Most likely, you can also find the company's web site address listed in any of its ads and promotional literature. If you still strike out, give the company a call—most will gladly give out their web address over the phone with no questions asked.

What will you find at a company web site? Usually, it contains information about the company's products or services. It may also give background on key personnel. Many corporate web sites list the company's job openings and allow you to apply online. You may also find press releases about recent noteworthy events at the company.

Another way to research a company is to search career web sites, some of which feature a section, called Employer Profiles, that gives detailed information on employers around the world. If the company in which you're interested is publicly held, check out its stock—information such as its general price range and recent history can help you assess how the company is doing.

A final way of learning about an individual company is to become familiar with its competitors. If you don't know offhand who they are, use search engines to find other companies in the same industry. Also, Hoover's Online (**www.hoovers.com**) is a first-rate resource. If a company is listed on Hoover's, often its competitors, and hyperlinks to their web sites, will be referenced.

Job openings databases.   Career sites download and index job postings every day. The organization of these databases allows you to search postings by location, job title, and required skills.

When using these databases, however, keep in mind that posted vacancies are sometimes out-of-date. Employers may forget to remove them once the position has been filled, or they may leave them online while the new hire is being "tried out." Other postings are sometimes designed merely to get information about job seekers into the databases of recruiters. Despite these drawbacks, employment databases are valuable job-searching tools (see the list of career sites at the end of this chapter).

Résumé banks.   You can enter your résumé into a data bank available to human resources professionals and recruiters. Don't get frustrated if you receive some responses that don't match your career objectives. Sometimes machines, not humans, match job openings to candidates.

Before posting your résumé to a particular data bank, be sure to investigate what type of employer would likely search that bank. Also, find out how long your résumé stays online. Most résumé banks provide this information on their web sites or answer specific questions by e-mail.

Online career discussion groups.   Discussion groups are online networks in which you exchange information with other job seekers and professionals through text messages. You enter a *chat room*, where you can ask questions, give and get advice, share war stories, exchange leads, and obtain information from specialists in different fields. To find a discussion group, use search engines or visit the major career sites listed at the end of this chapter.

Electronic bulletin boards.   Like a corkboard in your local grocery store or laundromat, these boards are for posting and reading notices. They contain thousands of help-wanted classifieds and enable job seekers to post their résumés. Most electronic bulletin boards charge nothing for their services; the few that charge nominal fees usually provide more services, such as categorizing your résumé for easy access to employers or ensuring confidentiality. Job listings are run by individuals, associations, civic groups, and corporations. There are a lot of listings, so be prepared to sift through them to find the ones relevant to your situation. To find these bulletin boards, visit some of the major career sites listed at the end of this chapter.

Newspaper classifieds.   With the Internet, you are no longer restricted to looking at classified ads only in your local newspaper. Many major newspapers, including the *New York Times, Washington Post, Chicago Tribune, Los Angeles Times,* and the *Boston Globe,* as well as many smaller newspapers, now post their classified employment ads online. Just go to the web site for the individual publication, and find the link to the classifieds section.

Additionally, some newspapers use the Internet to offer more details about jobs that appear in the print classified ads. That is, a classified ad in the newspaper might contain a Web ID code that you would use at the newspaper's web site to see an expanded listing. That listing should help you better identify opportunities that match your qualifications, write a more targeted cover letter, and prepare for an interview. The listing might also offer you a way to apply online.

Career guidance and job-search help.   Nearly all commercial online services and the Internet have areas devoted exclusively to helping job seekers manage their searches. These sites often include résumé templates, articles about job searching and career management, and discussion forums about careers (see the list of career sites at the end of this chapter).

Your own web site.   On your résumé and in your cover letters, you can refer to your personal home page—a great place to strut your stuff. The average size is usually four to twenty pages. Use your web site to give more detailed information about your background. Include work samples, photos, letters of recommendation, awards, and anything else that demonstrates to a prospective employer that you're the right person for the job. Many books and software packages are available to help you create your own web site, or you can enlist the services of a professional web designer.

E-mail.   Electronic-mail messages are a key component of modern communications, ranking with the telephone, traditional paper mail, and facsimile (fax) machines. One of the nice things about e-mail is that you can address your communication directly to an individual and have a good chance of it reaching him without interference from a secretary or other type of gatekeeper, because your e-mail goes straight to that individual's computer. Furthermore, you're more likely to receive a response to an e-mail than to other types of communication, because the professional is already seated at the computer and can dash off a quick, informal e-mail reply to your request.

E-mail is an excellent tool for finding out if a position has been filled, showing initial interest in a job, requesting more information, and inquiring about the status of a position you've applied for. It's fast, easy, and amazingly effective. To increase the chances that your e-mail will generate action, be sure it contains the following items: a statement that clearly identifies the purpose of the e-mail, relevant facts to support the purpose, a request specifying the next step to be taken, and a time frame in which you would appreciate a reply. Finally, don't forget to check your e-mail daily. A prospective employer who chooses to contact you by e-mail and does not get a fast response might go on to the next candidate.

Career products and services.   You can search through ads to locate products or services that might prove useful in your job search. Books about all aspects of job hunting, résumé software, career counselors, and networking services are just a few examples. Once again, use search engines and also the major career web sites to find the products and services you want.

Salary research.   Salary guides on the Internet can help you develop a realistic picture of what you might expect to earn in a particular profession. That information can be valuable to you when negotiating for a position. Many major career sites contain salary data.

Learning about a geographic area.   You can use the Internet to obtain data about a specific place you may be considering for relocation. For example, you can learn about the cost of living, housing options, and schools in that area.

Here's some advice for the hesitant: Don't be intimidated by computers and the Internet. Both are more user friendly than ever before. There are plenty of books that can help you get started if you need a little push. Also, the Internet has gained global acceptance, so one of your friends or teachers can no doubt offer advice or help. Don't put off using this valuable tool.

Searching the Internet

Finding the information you need on the Internet can be like searching for a needle in a haystack. Search engines are programs that help you do your research, acting almost like a card catalog in a library.

Literally hundreds of search engines exist. Some search the web at large, whereas others have a narrower focus and search a specific database. Not all search engines are created equal; they are specialists with different strengths and weaknesses. For this reason, it's important to perform your searches in more than one search engine.

Search engines have a search box, a space where you type in keywords or search phrases. To make your search more precise, use three or four keywords connected by *and*, rather than a single word. A single-word search can result in thousands of matches—more than you want to see. Almost every search engine has a help section that describes exactly how to get the best results. It's worth taking the time to read those directions. Some of the most widely used search engines are listed below:

- Google (**www.google.com**)
- AltaVista (**www.altavista.com**)
- AOL Anywhere (**www.aol.com**)
- Excite (**www.excite.com**)
- Galaxy (**www.galaxy.com**)
- HotBot (**www.hotbot.com**)
- Lycos (**www.lycos.com**)
- Yahoo! (**www.yahoo.com**)

The Right Site

Information on the Internet changes daily, even hourly, so sites listed here can quickly become obsolete. To get the most current information, you can do your own research online. Surfing the Internet is fun and educational.

You might also try your local bookstore or library. There are many books that, like traditional phone books, provide current Internet addresses, commonly referred to as URLs (Universal Resource Locators).

In the interest of getting you started, here are the URLs for some of the top sites related to job hunting and careers, valid at the time of this book's publication:

- America's CareerInfoNet—**www.acinet.org**
- America's Employers—**www.americasemployers.com**
- America's Job Bank—**www.ajb.dni.us**
- Careerbuilder—**www.careerbuilder.com**
- Careermag.com—**www.careermag.com**
- Careers OnLine—**www.careersonline.com**
- CareerShop—**www.careershop.com**
- CareerSite.com—**www.careersite.com**
- HotJobs—**www.hotjobs.com**
- Monster.com—**www.monster.com**
- Monstertrak—**www.monstertrak.com**

Filling Out Job Applications

Learning Objectives

In this chapter, you will learn how to do the following:

- Properly complete a job application form
- Answer typical application questions

Chapter 11

STRATEGIES
in ACTION

John walked into the main office of the manufacturing company, résumé in hand. He had an interview appointment with a representative from the Human Resources Department to discuss an accounting position. Before calling the person with whom John was to meet, the receptionist handed John an application to complete.

John sat down and pulled from his folder a practice application that he'd prepared before the interview. On it, he had listed all the information about his previous employment as well as his educational background. Now, completing the real job application was a piece of cake—he simply copied the relevant information from his practice application. Because he was prepared, he was able to fill in all the blanks quickly and not worry about making a mistake or accidentally omitting something important. In just a few moments, he was able to return the completed application to the receptionist and let her know he was ready to meet the interviewer.

The Application Form

Many companies require a completed application form as well as a résumé from candidates before interviewing them. Completing an application form isn't difficult. Nonetheless, it's important to do it right. Take the task as seriously as you would any of the other aspects of job hunting by being prepared, giving thought to your answers, and presenting your information in a neat, concise manner.

Completing the Blanks

It's essential to follow certain general rules when completing an application form, to avoid being eliminated from the field of contenders.

1. **Write in pen.** Pencil smudges look unprofessional. Be prepared and bring a pen with you.

2. **Print clearly.** Imagine the frustration of an employer who is interested in your application but cannot decipher your name or phone number.

3. **Use one lettering style.** You can print or use script, whichever form of your penmanship is neater, but be sure to stick with your choice throughout the application.

4. **Complete every line.** If a section is not applicable, write "n/a" or draw a line through the answer space. Check the side, top, and bottom margins and both sides of the paper for questions you might have missed.

5. **Know your work history.** Bring with you, on an index card or a practice application, the names, addresses, and phone numbers of all your former employers, plus a list of people to contact as references. If your experience is limited, it is perfectly acceptable to include names of people for whom you've done odd jobs, such as yard work or baby-sitting.

6. **Choose references carefully.** Before you begin filling out job applications, it is a good idea to call or write the people you wish to serve as references for you, to ask their permission and to remind them of your current career goals. Do not list anyone from whom you have the least bit of doubt about getting a good reference. You may not have much space on the form, but an ideal mix would be two to three professional references who could discuss the quality of your work and one to two personal references (not relatives) who could discuss your character.

7. **Be careful when giving salary requirements.** If possible, avoid committing yourself to a specific number. An amount that is too high could eliminate you, and an amount that is too low could cost you if you're hired. If you must indicate a desired salary, research the going rate in your field and give a salary range that would be acceptable to you.

8. **Use only recognizable abbreviations.** This will help maximize the readability of your application.

9. **Be neat.** Remember that the attention you show to your application reflects how you will perform on the job. Messy scratch-outs and missed questions leave a bad impression.

10. **Be courteous to everyone you meet at the job location.** Many people who go to job sites to fill out applications assume that because the application visit isn't a formal interview, they can be casual, rude, or unprepared. Remember that your first contact with an employer creates a strong impression. Dress as you would for a job interview. Be friendly and courteous—even to those whom you might consider "unimportant," such as clerks and secretaries. These people may have input in the hiring decision and could end up being your coworkers.

11. **Proofread.** In the rush of job hunting, it is easy to become nervous and careless. Show the employer that you pay attention to detail by handing in an application that represents a job well done.

Typical Application Questions

Although every job application form is different, there are many questions that are fairly common. Review the following list to better prepare your answers.

1. **Name.** Follow instructions in filling out this blank. Applications often require you to place your last name first and to include your middle initial.

2. **Address.** Give your entire address, including your ZIP code.

Fill out job applications with care. A neat, properly completed form can help make a good first impression. (© Dion Ogust/The Image Works)

3. **Phone number.** Be sure that the phone you list will always be answered, even if by an answering machine.

4. **Social Security number.** Your Social Security number often becomes your employee identification number, which companies then use to input and retrieve your file from their system. Be sure you write down the number accurately.

5. **Person to reach in case of emergency.** Name a person who can be reached during your work hours and who can respond quickly in an emergency situation, preferably someone local with his or her own transportation.

6. **Citizenship.** The employer asks for this information to ensure you are a U.S. citizen or an alien who has a legal right to hold the job for which you are applying.

7. **Position you are applying for.** Be as specific as possible in naming the type of job you seek. Use the correct title of the job if you know it.

8. **Salary desired.** Unless you know the exact salary being offered for the job you want, it is best to give a range that leaves you some room for negotiation. You may also use phrases such as "to be discussed" or "negotiable," if you think it would be to your benefit to avoid listing a figure.

9. **Date available.** Give the earliest possible date you could begin a job. If you are currently unemployed, write "immediately." If you are employed, give a date that allows for at least a two-week notice period at your current job.

10. **Education.** List your high school, college, graduate school, and any specialized courses or certifications you've completed.

11. **Work experience.** Have this information prepared before you begin filling out the application form. You'll need to include the names of previous employers and their addresses and phone numbers as well as your job title, dates of employment, and supervisor's name. You may also be asked your reasons for leaving former jobs. Present your responses in a positive light—for example, "Was ready for new challenges and additional responsibility."

12. **Military service.** List your military experience, or write "n/a" if it is not applicable.

13. **Have you ever been convicted of a crime?** Answer honestly. Many employers routinely check for criminal records. If an employer hires you and then learns you lied, you will be fired.

14. **Hobbies or interests.** Use this area to call attention to any of your specific interests that might make you a more valuable employee or demonstrate you have a well-rounded personality.

15. **Foreign language ability.** List the languages (other than English) that you know. You may also be asked to assess your proficiency in reading, writing, and speaking the foreign languages you list.

16. **References.** List previous employers, teachers, or other professional contacts. Be prepared to provide their phone numbers and addresses. Do not use relatives. Character references need to have known you for at least two years.

17. **Signature and date.** This line is important! Your signature and the date confirm that you have, to the best of your knowledge, completed the questions accurately. An application is not considered valid unless it is signed and dated.

18. **For personnel use only.** Check out this section to get a hint about the kinds of information the prospective employer will seek in an interview.

EXERCISE   A sample employment application appears on the following pages. Fill it out for practice and to create a master document with all your relevant information. Refer to it when completing actual employment applications.

APPLICATION FOR EMPLOYMENT

PRE-EMPLOYMENT QUESTIONNAIRE
EQUAL OPPORTUNITY EMPLOYER

PERSONAL INFORMATION

DATE _____

NAME (LAST NAME FIRST)	SOCIAL SECURITY NO.

PRESENT ADDRESS	CITY	STATE	ZIP CODE

PERMANENT ADDRESS	CITY	STATE	ZIP CODE

PHONE NO. ( )	REFERRED BY

EMPLOYMENT DESIRED

POSITION	DATE YOU CAN START	SALARY DESIRED

ARE YOU EMPLOYED? ☐ YES ☐ NO	IF SO, MAY WE INQUIRE OF YOUR PRESENT EMPLOYER? ☐ YES ☐ NO

EVER APPLIED TO THIS COMPANY BEFORE? ☐ YES ☐ NO	WHERE?	WHEN?

EDUCATION HISTORY

	NAME & LOCATION OF SCHOOL	YEARS ATTENDED	DID YOU GRADUATE?	SUBJECTS STUDIED
GRAMMAR SCHOOL				
HIGH SCHOOL				
COLLEGE				
TRADE, BUSINESS OR CORRESPONDENCE SCHOOL				

GENERAL INFORMATION

SUBJECTS OF SPECIAL STUDY/RESEARCH WORK OR SPECIAL TRAINING/SKILLS

U.S. MILITARY OR NAVAL SERVICE	RANK

FORMER EMPLOYERS (LIST BELOW LAST FOUR EMPLOYERS, STARTING WITH LAST ONE FIRST)

DATE MONTH AND YEAR	NAME & ADDRESS OF EMPLOYER	SALARY	POSITION	REASON FOR LEAVING
FROM				
TO				
FROM				
TO				
FROM				
TO				
FROM				
TO				

APPLICATION FOR EMPLOYMENT

CONTINUED ON OTHER SIDE

REFERENCES   GIVE BELOW THE NAMES OF THREE PERSONS NOT RELATED TO YOU, WHOM YOU HAVE KNOWN AT LEAST ONE YEAR.

NAME	ADDRESS	BUSINESS	YEARS KNOWN

AUTHORIZATION

"I certify that the facts contained in this application are true and complete to the best of my knowledge and understand that, if employed, falsified statements on this application shall be grounds for dismissal.

I authorize investigation of all statements contained herein and the references and employers listed above to give you any and all information concerning my previous employment and any pertinent information they may have, personal or otherwise, and release the company from all liability for any damage that may result from utilization of such information.

I also understand and agree that no representative of the company has any authority to enter into any agreement for employment for any specified period of time, or to make any agreement contrary to the foregoing, unless it is in writing and signed by an authorized company representative."

DATE _____ SIGNATURE _____

INTERVIEWED BY _____ DATE _____

———————————————— DO NOT WRITE BELOW THIS LINE ————————————————

REMARKS

NEATNESS		CHARACTER		
PERSONALITY		ABILITY		
HIRED	FOR DEPT.	POSITION	WILL REPORT	SALARY WAGES

APPROVED: 1. _____ 2. _____ 3. _____
EMPLOYMENT MANAGER   DEPARTMENT HEAD   GENERAL MANAGER

Interviewing

Learning Objectives

In this chapter, you will learn to do the following:

- Prepare for interviews
- Create a good first impression
- Handle interview stress
- Answer typical interview questions
- Examine your personality
- Pay attention to body language
- Follow up on an interview
- Create a career-search organization chart
- Avoid making major interview gaffes
- Handle rejection
- Ask for what you want

Chapter 12

STRATEGIES in ACTION

Peggy sat in the lobby waiting for her name to be called. She'd already given her name to the receptionist. Now it would be just a matter of minutes before she met the prospective employer considering her for a position in the company's Information Technology Department.

Peggy reviewed in her mind all the steps she'd gone through to prepare for this interview. She'd researched the company extensively in the library and online. She'd conducted informational interviews with people in the field. She'd done two practice interviews with girlfriends, perfecting her answers to their questions about her work history and related experience. She'd even practiced shaking hands and making good eye contact.

Last night, Peggy had done a complete dress rehearsal, trying on her interview outfit to be sure it was appropriate, fit comfortably, and was perfectly ironed. She had also assembled all her interview materials—including her resume, some letters of recommendation from previous employers, and a draft of a job application to help her remember dates and phone numbers should she have to complete an application for the job.

Peggy waited, relaxed and confident that she truly was ready for the interview.

Preparing for Interviews

Many people are underprepared for interviewing and therefore more nervous than they need to be. Think of an interview as a three-step process, and plan the execution of each step. Remember that you have only a short time to convey your experience, potential, and personality to an interviewer.

As you go through the interview process, envision the person with whom you'll be interviewing. Most likely this individual will be of a different generation or background than you. Keep in mind that she may have conservative expectations about your dress and conduct. Dress and act not as if you were with one of your peers, but rather with someone who holds you to a higher standard.

Prepare for the different types of interviewers you may encounter. Applicants are often interviewed first by a human resources manager, then by a department manager or direct supervisor. Sometimes two or three people conduct the interview together.

As a job hunter, your goal is to get to the person to whom you'd be reporting. Remember that human resources representatives often function as screeners, with the purpose of weeding people out. In some cases, human resources people have only a general knowledge of the available position; they may also be reluctant to describe the people with whom you'd be working most closely. Your objective is to either bypass the human resources department or be impressive enough to make it to the next step: your future supervisor.

Use the following guidelines to prepare for interviews. Review them frequently during your job search.

Before the Interview

1. Dress properly (to ensure that the interviewer remembers you, not your clothes).

2. Be on time.

3. Research the organization—what it does and its projects, future plans, size, and problems. Start with the company's web site and annual report.

4. Be prepared to ask questions—you're interviewing the employer, too!

5. Bring your résumé and examples of past performance.

6. Practice your responses.
   a. Role-play interviewing with a friend.
   b. Think through your answers aloud while you're driving or in front of the mirror at home.
   c. Paraphrase. To show you're a good listener, practice rephrasing in your own words the information given by the interviewer in your role-play exercise.

During the Interview

1. Give a positive, initial greeting. Use a firm handshake and display a positive attitude.

2. Be truthful, but never put yourself down.

3. Speak distinctly.

4. Help the interviewer.
   a. Explain your experiences and skills.
   b. Relate your experiences and skills to the job for which you're interviewing.

5. Don't be too serious or too humorous.

6. Listen carefully and make good eye contact.

7. Be concise.

8. Do not oversell yourself.

After the Interview (often neglected but vital steps)

1. Write down information and discussion points about the organization and the job.

2. Evaluate your interview; determine how to improve your next one.

3. Write thank-you letters.

4. Follow up with phone calls to determine the status of the hiring decision.

Types of Interviews

Not all interviews are alike. You can prevent surprises by preparing for the different types of interviews. With proper preparation, you'll be able to demonstrate your skills and convey your personality effectively in any type of interview.

Behavioral or Situational Interviews

An increasingly popular type of interview, the behavioral or situational interview is based on the premise that your past performance is the best predictor of your future performance. The interviewer typically asks very specific, probing questions to tease out your past behaviors. The candidate's job is to briefly and specifically explain past situations, actions taken, and results achieved.

Board Interviews

In board interviews, the candidate meets with several interviewers in a formal setting. These interviews are most often used for hiring at the corporate level, where several people may want to be directly involved in the decision process. Board interviews require special preparation and forethought.

Directed Interviews

In directed interviews, the interviewer follows a definite set of questions. You may notice that the interviewer has a checklist. Directed interviews are usually used to prescreen applicants for another interview.

Group Interviews

An interviewer may ask the job candidate to work with others on a particular task or topic. Observers note your leadership abilities and skill at working as part of a team. Group interviews require special preparation and forethought.

Informational Interviews

Some job hunters use this type of interview to gain information from a person who works in a field of interest to them. This is the only type of interview in which the candidate does not ask for a job at the end of the session. (See the section on informational interviews on page 37.)

Meal Interviews

Held in a more casual setting, the breakfast, lunch, or dinner interview allows the interviewer and applicant to more easily develop a rapport. In such an interview, follow the host's lead in ordering food and in business etiquette, remembering that all other interview rules still apply.

Nondirected Interviews

Nondirected interviews are less structured and less formal than other types of interviews. Not surprisingly, they are often used in informal workplaces. Nondirected interviews may allow more room for expression. The questions asked tend to be open-ended and spontaneous.

Stress Interviews

Stress interviews are designed to see how well a job candidate holds up under pressure. If the position you're applying for involves a great deal of stress, don't be surprised to encounter a high-pressure interviewer. Even interviewers for non-stressful jobs may try to shake your poise by using rapid-fire or tricky questions. Recognize this type of interview for what it is—a test, and consider whether you'd feel comfortable working for an employer who uses this interviewing method.

Telephone Interviews

Telephone interviews may involve a combination of different interviewing techniques. For example, you may be interviewed by one person or by a group. Telephone interviews are typically used to screen out applicants, although they may also be used as a follow-up to an earlier conversation. The job hunter's primary goal in this type of interview is to secure a face-to-face meeting.

EXERCISE

Preparation Worksheet

If you think through your skills, you will be better prepared to explain them to the interviewer and to relate them to the position you want.

Past Job, Hobby, or Volunteer Work   *Skill I Learned/Value to Employer*

1. _____   1. _____

   _____   _____

2. _____   2. _____

   _____   _____

3. _____   3. _____

   _____   _____

4. _____   4. _____

   _____   _____

5. _____   5. _____

   _____   _____

Here is an alternative way to organize your thoughts before an interview.

My Strongest Skills	*Where I Developed My Strongest Skills/Examples*
1. _____ _____	1. _____ _____
2. _____ _____	2. _____ _____
3. _____ _____	3. _____ _____
4. _____ _____	4. _____ _____
5. _____ _____	5. _____ _____

Create a Good First Impression

Studies have shown that people form an opinion of someone they meet in the first two to four minutes. For that reason, it is vital that you pay attention to detail to create the best possible first impression. Some factors that affect the impression you make are your age, sex, appearance (hair, clothes, hygiene, jewelry, makeup), movement, mannerisms, personal space, and manner of speaking. Good manners also play an important role.

Rules of Business Etiquette

To enhance the likelihood of making a favorable impression, follow these basic rules:

1. Arrive on time or five minutes early.

2. Introduce yourself politely to the receptionist and state the first and last names of the individual you are to see.

3. If the receptionist offers coffee or tea, you may accept it, but be sure you won't have trouble juggling the cup and your résumé materials when you shake hands with the interviewer. It might be best to politely pass on the offer.

4. If you accept a soft drink from the receptionist or your interviewer, pour it into a cup, if available, rather than drinking it from the can.

5. Do not chew gum.

6. Do not smoke. It is also best not to smoke just before an interview, as many people find the residual smell offensive.

7. Introduce yourself to the interviewer by clearly stating both your first and last names. Make eye contact and smile.

8. Say something to the effect of "It's nice to meet you" in your initial greeting.

9. Address the interviewer as Mr. _____ or Ms. _____ unless you are asked to do otherwise. Don't assume that if the interviewer calls you by your first name you are both on a first-name basis.

10. Be willing to make a bit of small talk, possibly about the weather, the traffic on the way to the interview, or the interviewer's good directions.

11. After the interviewer has led you from the reception area to an office or conference room, do not take a seat until the interviewer motions you to a particular place.

12. Sit straight and relatively still. Avoid distracting movements of your hands or legs.

13. Fold your hands comfortably in your lap or on top of your résumé materials. Do not cross your arms over your chest (you will appear disagreeable) or spread them across the back of the chair or couch (you will appear too relaxed, lazy, or uninterested).

14. Be attentive when the interviewer speaks. Avoid interrupting, even if the interviewer does most of the talking. Maintain good eye contact with the interviewer.

15. Don't hesitate to ask for clarification if you don't understand something.

16. Be positive and upbeat in your remarks.

17. Avoid complaining about a previous job or employer. Even if your remarks are true, you won't appear professional if you harp on these subjects.

18. Avoid criticizing, contradicting, or disagreeing with the interviewer.

19. If you are offered a tour of the facility, the interviewer will indicate whether you are to walk ahead or to follow. Women should know that male interviewers often encourage them to pass through doorways first.

20. At the end of the meeting, thank the interviewer for his time and extend your hand for a strong parting handshake. Don't forget to smile and make eye contact one last time.

Dress to Impress

As a job hunter, you need to keep in mind that people form first impressions quickly, and first impressions are lasting. Consequently, your dress should be understated, conservative, and neat. A good rule of thumb is to dress slightly better than you would to report to the job every day. For example, for a job interview at a workplace where blue jeans are acceptable garb, you could wear casual slacks.

How do you determine the dress code in your intended workplace? Do research. Ask around. If it's a public place, such as a bank or restaurant, drop by and observe before the day of your interview. If you're still unsure, a suit in a dark or neutral color is almost always a good choice. Wear something you've worn at least once before, to be certain you'll feel comfortable and confident. Of course, avoid any clothing that is visibly worn, torn, or wrinkled.

Here are some other details about dress that can leave an interviewer with a poor impression.

Women should avoid:

- Exposed tattoos or body piercings.

- Hair that is too styled, overteased, or overmoussed. Keep hair conservatively styled.

- Dangly earrings, or too many earrings, rings, necklaces, or bracelets.

- Too much makeup or perfume. Too little is always better than too much.

- Low-cut or unbuttoned blouses or any sign of an undergarment (straps or anything that would show through a sheer blouse or skirt). Going braless is a definite no-no.

- Bare legs.

- Patterned nylons. Plain, sheer hose are best.

- Tight, short, or leather or suede skirts.

- Trendy or faddish accessories.

- Lots of ruffles, bows, or fringe. Remember that you want to appear business-like and professional.

- Very high heels or glittery, silver or gold shoes.

Men should avoid:

- Exposed tattoos or body piercings.

- Long, unkempt hair. Wear hair short or tie it back and keep it conservatively styled.

- Earrings, bracelets, pinkie rings, or similar jewelry.

- Too much aftershave or cologne.

- Unbuttoned shirts.

- T-shirts or patterned T-shirts under dress shirts.

- White socks or socks that clash with slacks.

- Sheer or white slacks.

- Novelty ties or leather ties.

- Sneakers or sandals.

- Cargo pants or excessively baggy pants.

It's often helpful to have a "dress rehearsal" the evening before a job interview. First, this gives you the opportunity to find missing buttons or fallen hems
while you can still fix them. Second, you can ask the opinion of a good friend or
relative. Finally, you'll see your put-together, professional self, which should build
confidence and poise for the interview.

EXERCISE   Choose a day to wear your interview clothes to class. Ask your classmates or instructor for feedback. Can they guess your desired career field or position? What do they
notice first? Solicit constructive criticism. Make notes about this for future interviews.

Presenting Yourself on the Telephone

Your initial phone call to a potential employer can often make the difference between getting an interview and being overlooked as a candidate for a job.

When your first contact with an employer is by telephone, be sure to be courteous to whomever answers the phone. Support staff often decide whether calls
should be put through, and in today's lean, customer-service-oriented companies,
it is not uncommon for supervisors themselves to answer the phone.

One trick for calling difficult-to-reach executives is to try early in the morning
or after 5:00 P.M. Typically, managers are at work at these times but their secretaries are not, so they are more likely to answer the phone. In general, it's best to
make calls in the morning, when people are alert and not yet immersed in the
day's events.

Telephone Etiquette

1. **Be prepared.** Know to whom you want to speak and what you want to say.
   You may want to practice your presentation, but try not to sound too re-
   hearsed when you finally place your call. Clear away distractions. Crying children in the background or television or kitchen noise detract from your
   professionalism. Set a goal for the phone call, such as to obtain an interview
   appointment or establish an initial contact.

2. **Ask politely but authoritatively for the person you want to reach.** If you
   sound hesitant or unsure of yourself, you may have difficulty getting past the

secretary. If you were referred by a mutual contact, give that person's name to the secretary, to help ensure that your call is put through.

3. **Offer to call back if the person is unavailable.** Executives often do not return unsolicited calls from job hunters. Ask the secretary to recommend a good time for you to try again. After a few attempts, try leaving a message. State your first and last names, the reason you're calling, your phone number, and the best time to reach you. Don't be personally insulted if your call is not returned—this is often standard operating procedure. By being politely persistent and calling again, your efforts eventually may be rewarded.

4. **When you do eventually get through to the person you want, give a quick greeting, identify yourself using both your first and last names, and briefly state why you're calling.** Every conversation differs, of course, so you'll need to vary your approach. In an ideal situation, you'll have a receptive listener on the other end of the line. Begin by highlighting your assets, explaining how your skills match the company's needs. Briefly mention some of your successes or specific accomplishments at a previous job or in school. Pause when appropriate to allow the person to provide feedback and ask questions.

Telephone Goals

Your most likely goal is an in-person meeting, so you needn't insist on an extensive telephone interview. Hiring decisions are rarely, if ever, made over the phone. Ask for an interview by saying something like: "I've enjoyed speaking with you. Is there a convenient time we could get together and talk further in person?"

If the person suggests you send in your résumé, agree to put one in the mail and attempt again to set a time for a follow-up meeting. If the response is still negative, thank the individual for talking with you. Explain that you will send the résumé and will follow up with another call in a week or so, after she has had time to review it.

Make sure you keep a list of whom you've called, when you called, and what the next action is to be. Calling back when you say you will is an easy way of demonstrating that you are serious about a position and that you are dependable.

The Telephone Interview

As mentioned earlier, some employers use the phone to carry out interviews or to conduct preliminary "meetings." Usually, phone interviews happen in one of three ways:

1. You cold-call the prospective employer to get information about job availability, and he begins asking you interview questions because you arouse his interest.

2. A company calls you unexpectedly as a response to a letter and/or résumé you sent.

3. You or a placement agency set up a specific time for a telephone interview.

No matter how the interview comes about, the bottom line is the same—a prospective employer is interested in you. It's vital that you seize the opportunity to get to the next step, an in-person meeting. Therefore, the telephone interview becomes a trial run for the real thing.

Effective telephone interviews, like face-to-face meetings, require preparation. Because you never know when a company might call you once your networking process is under way, you should keep a file of companies you've contacted next to the phone. Be sure the file is organized (alphabetical order by company name usually works best) so that you can quickly locate a copy of the materials you sent the caller as well as any research you may have done about the company.

The most important point to remember is that phone interviews usually represent a weeding-out process. The interviewer is listening for any indication that you might *not* be the right person for the job or that it would be a waste of time to arrange a face-to-face meeting. Here are some tips to help you succeed in a phone interview.

1. **Take a surprise call in stride.** Even though the call may come at the most inopportune time, try to sound pleased, friendly, and collected.

2. **Let the interviewer do most of the talking.** Keep your answers to the interviewer's questions brief and to the point. Rambling will bore the interviewer. However, try to avoid giving yes or no answers—they don't provide information about your abilities.

3. **Don't hesitate to ask some of your own questions.** This is an excellent opportunity to learn more about the company and the position in question. The information you gain will help you decide if you're interested in the job and, if so, will prove useful when you prepare for an in-person interview. Under no circumstances, however, should you ask about money or vacation time; these inquiries would be premature and inappropriate. Your focus should be on the responsibilities of the position.

4. **Speak clearly into the telephone.** Don't eat, drink, or smoke while on the phone. Turn down any background music, and eliminate other background noises as much as possible.

5. **Take notes of your conversation.** Keep a pen and paper close to the phone at all times, just for this purpose. Jot down any relevant information the interviewer gives you about the position. You may also need to write down a meeting time and directions to the location of your in-person interview.

6. **Get a name and phone number.** If you have been invited to meet with the interviewer, write down her name and phone number so that you can make contact should you have to change the appointment for any reason.

7. **Anticipate dialogue.** Rehearse your responses to possible questions. Create cue cards as prompts.

8. **Avoid salary issues.** If pressed, present a wide salary range that is acceptable to you, noting that you do not yet know enough about the position or its demands to be more specific.

9. **Try to reschedule if necessary.** Surprise interviews are difficult even for the most seasoned job hunter. If the call comes at an inconvenient time, see if you can make an appointment for another time, so that you can prepare your notes and create a calm and productive interview setting.

10. **Push for a face-to-face interview.** Ask something like, "May we discuss this further next Tuesday afternoon?"

11. **Express thanks.** Close the conversation with appreciation for the caller's interest.

Remember that your single objective at this point is to sell yourself, so that the interviewer requests an in-person meeting. It is unlikely you will be offered a position after only a phone interview. If the interviewer does not suggest a face-to-face meeting, take the initiative to ask for one. You have nothing to lose.

It is difficult to evaluate an opportunity over the phone. Even if the job doesn't sound right, go to the interview to get the practice. It may happen that the job sounds better when you get all the facts or that you learn of a more suitable position elsewhere within the company.

How to Handle Interview Stress

Many people consider a job interview to be one of life's most stressful events. Some become so overwhelmed that they sabotage their own success. If you feel overly threatened by job interviews, try the exercises described in the following sections.

Put Things into Perspective

Some people place so much importance on each interview that the pressure to succeed becomes crippling. When you catch yourself thinking terrifying thoughts that start with the word *if,* stop and redirect yourself. "If" thoughts have a tendency to pile up and weigh you down.

A nonproductive train of thought might proceed this way: "*If* I don't do well at this interview, I'll be so disappointed. I'll never have the confidence to do well at another interview." Another might be: "*If* I don't land this job, my parents (spouse, friends) will think I'm such a failure. How will I pay for the rent (car, mortgage)?" These thoughts are self-defeating and negative. They focus on the future, which you can't control, at the expense of the present, which you can control.

Instead of terrorizing yourself with "what *if*s," be your own best friend. Say nothing to yourself that you wouldn't say to a good friend to whom you were trying to lend confidence. Say everything to yourself that you'd say to a friend who needed a little extra support going into a stressful situation.

Instead of thinking:

What *if* I become tongue-tied during the interview and ruin my chances?

Tell yourself:

Of course it's natural for me to feel nervous at first, but I'm sure I'll relax and do fine.

EXERCISE

In the spaces below, write down a few positive, calming, and confidence-producing thoughts. (If you have trouble doing this, think of things you would say to a good friend.)

Positive Statements

1. _____

   _____

2. _____

   _____

3. _____

   _____

If you need to, read these over just before you go to interviews. Why should you give yourself any less support and respect than you would your best friend?

Sweaty Palms Are Not a Crime

Sometimes, even though you succeed in calming your stressful thoughts, your body does not cooperate. Sweaty palms, a nervous stomach, and a dry mouth are symptoms occasionally felt by nervous job hunters. Don't let this type of physical discomfort throw you. Try the relaxation techniques listed below.

1. **Use nature's original relaxation device: the sigh.** Allow yourself a few huge sighs and notice how tension leaves your body.

2. **Focus on your breathing.** While sitting in a waiting room, take long, slow, deep breaths through your nose. If you have the opportunity, close your eyes, sit comfortably, and imagine that your breath has a color. In your mind's eye, watch your breath as it enters and leaves your body. The resulting deep breaths will prevent you from focusing on nervous thoughts, relax your muscles, and oxygenate your brain. (Try it now and see.)

3. **Slowly and sequentially, tense and release each muscle group in your body.** Start with your toes and work up to your head. Some people also imagine their body as a vessel filled with warm sunshine.

Bookstores and libraries offer many books about relaxation techniques. Information can also be found on the Internet. Do some research to find a few tricks that work for you.

Remember that stress is not all bad. We all need a little stress to be productive. Think of adrenaline as an asset. Why not use the extra zip to project more energy, think clearly, and speak distinctly? Focus on the ways stress can work *for* you and not *against* you.

EXERCISE

Do You Have Interview Anxiety?

	Never	Sometimes	Always
Before an interview:			
I have trouble sleeping.	❑	❑	❑
I get a headache.	❑	❑	❑
I get a stomachache.	❑	❑	❑
I lose my appetite.	❑	❑	❑
My palms sweat.	❑	❑	❑
I have canceled an interview because of panic.	❑	❑	❑
In an interview:			
My hands shake.	❑	❑	❑
I have trouble remembering things.	❑	❑	❑
My mind keeps going blank.	❑	❑	❑
I tap my hands or feet constantly.	❑	❑	❑
I crack my knuckles frequently.	❑	❑	❑
I can't think clearly.	❑	❑	❑
I can't wait to get out of the room.	❑	❑	❑
I feel nervous and jittery.	❑	❑	❑
I worry that I'm doing poorly.	❑	❑	❑
I have a hard time understanding directions.	❑	❑	❑
I can't remember things I said.	❑	❑	❑
I feel like crying.	❑	❑	❑
I feel exhausted.	❑	❑	❑

Tally your check marks. If you have more than five checks in the Sometimes or Always columns, plan a strategy for extra interview practice.

Hide Your Nervousness

All interviewers expect interviewees to be a little nervous. You don't want your nervous actions to detract from your appearance and the impression you make, however. By becoming aware of the nervous signals you give off, you'll be able to eliminate them and present yourself more confidently in interviews. See if you find yourself exhibiting any of the following behaviors:

- Playing with your hair
- Wringing your hands
- Cracking your knuckles
- Clearing your throat
- Tugging at your ear
- Playing with your jewelry
- Touching your neck
- Picking or pinching your skin
- Jingling money in your pocket
- Covering your mouth with your hands when you speak
- Tapping your hands, feet, or pen
- Swiveling in your chair

EXERCISE   Do a mock interview with a friend while a silent third person looks on outside your line of vision. (Better yet, videotape yourself!) Have the observer take notes, listing any nervous signals you display.

Once you've identified (or viewed on video) the ways your anxiety manifests itself, focus on eliminating these tendencies and continue to practice your interview skills at home. The best remedy, however, is simply doing as many interviews as you can, even for jobs in which you are not that interested. The real-world practice you receive from these interviews will help you perfect your presentation, gain self-confidence, and eventually minimize, if not altogether eliminate, your feelings of anxiety.

Questions Asked in Job Interviews

Although every interview will, of course, be different, you can still prepare. Think of the movie stars and politicians you often see interviewed on television or in magazines and newspapers. You can be sure that most of their answers are at least somewhat scripted. Although their delivery might seem natural, there's no doubt that they've given thought to the questions they might be asked and the best possible answers to them. Learn from the experts, and carefully plan this important aspect of the job-hunting process.

EXERCISE

Questions an Interviewer Might Ask You

As always, practice makes perfect. Read the following list of questions, and answer them aloud. This exercise will lessen your chances of being caught off-guard in an actual interview.

1. Tell me about yourself.
2. What is your grade point average?
3. What is your major?
4. What courses do you enjoy in college?
5. What courses don't you enjoy?
6. What do you know about our organization?
7. What can you do for us? Why should we hire you?
8. What qualifications do you have that make you feel you will be successful in your field?
9. How did you hear about this position?
10. What types of jobs have you had in the past?
11. What have you learned from the jobs you've held?
12. Have you participated in any volunteer or community work? What did you learn from those experiences?
13. How do you feel about routine work?
14. What are your future vocational plans?
15. If you could write your own ticket, what would be your dream job?
16. Are you willing to travel?
17. What have you done that shows initiative and willingness to work?
18. Are you involved in any extracurricular activities?
19. Do you hold any positions of leadership at school?
20. What are your special skills, and how did you acquire them?
21. Are there any work or school achievements you are particularly proud of?
22. Why did you leave your most recent job?
23. Do you have any geographical restrictions or preferences?

24. How do you spend your spare time? What are your hobbies?

25. What percentage of your college expenses did you earn? How?

26. What do you consider to be your strengths? Your weaknesses?

27. What books have you read recently?

28. If you were fired from a previous job, what was the reason?

29. Discuss five major accomplishments in your lifetime.

30. When can you start work?

31. When can you visit our headquarters for further interviews?

32. What kind of boss would you like?

33. If you could spend a day with someone you've known or known of, who would it be?

34. What personality characteristics rub you the wrong way?

35. Define *cooperation*.

36. How do you show your anger? What types of things make you angry?

37. Have you ever quit any activities? If so, what were they?

38. Have you ever experienced discrimination?

39. What does "9 to 5" mean to you?

40. With what type of person do you spend the majority of your time?

41. What questions do you have for me?

Remember that "questions" can take many forms. You may be asked to perform a task during an interview—anything from composing a letter to working on a project. Be prepared to demonstrate your expertise.

How to Respond to Interview Questions

After reviewing the list of possible interview questions, you may become confused as to how to respond. First, remember to be truthful, but not self-deprecating. If you need to discuss an area of weakness, do so, but follow up immediately with your plan for addressing that weakness. Second, practice, practice, practice. Rehearsing your responses will enable you to answer readily and prepare you to highlight your strong points. It will also reduce your level of nervousness. Some of the questions in the list require special reflection about why an employer would ask them in the first place. Below are some of the questions job hunters find most difficult and some strategies for answering them.

Tell me about yourself.   This is perhaps the most common of all interview questions. Don't view it as vague and intimidating, but as a gift. After all, there are no wrong answers, and this question presents you with the opportunity to begin the interview by presenting your most important strengths. The interviewer is trying to determine what kind of person you are and is leaving the parameters of that definition up to you.

Think of your three strongest qualifications for the job at hand and begin by listing those. For example, "I am a recent graduate of _____ University, and I have recently completed an internship with a company in this field. I've also lived in this area for the past ten years and have a good sense of the local economy." Or, "I'm a mature employee with fifteen years' work experience. I have strong work habits and ethics, and I have recent training in the software used in this field." If the interviewer seems to be waiting for a more complete response, follow up with, "Does that answer your question?"

What courses did you enjoy/not enjoy in college?   This question is another way of asking, "What are you good at?" or "Would you be happy performing the duties that are integral to this position?" If you can do so honestly, list the courses that relate to your intended position. If you enjoyed courses that strengthened your communication or technical skills, be sure to list those as well. Keep the list of courses you didn't enjoy small. Every manager fears hiring a negative person with a long list of dislikes.

What types of jobs have you held in the past? What did you learn from them?   Or, more aptly put, *did* you learn? Many interviewers are not as troubled by a job hunter who has held fairly menial jobs in the past as they are by one who has not learned any new skills from past experiences and therefore brings little to the new job. To respond to these questions, briefly list the areas of your former jobs, but spend the most time explaining your transferable skills. An example would be: "I worked my way through college as a server in a local restaurant, and I learned a lot about working under pressure and interacting with the public." Of course, if you have held jobs in a field related to the one in which you are applying, it would be appropriate to explain your specific skills in detail.

What books have you read recently? What are your hobbies?   The worst possible answer to the first question is: *"Books?"* Questions such as these seek to ascertain whether you are a bright, well-rounded individual whose personality will fit on the employer's team. Answer simply and honestly. There are no wrong types of books or hobbies, as long as you do indeed name some. Do be careful to avoid mention of any political, religious, or controversial topics that could be used to discriminate against you, however.

What can you do for us? Why should we hire you? What do you know about this organization?   These questions evaluate your knowledge of yourself, the company, and the position. Answer by describing a few things about the company, such as how large they are or what they do, and then explaining how your skills would fit the company's needs. The more homework you've done on the company and on identifying your own skills, the easier it will be to answer these questions. Express confidence in your abilities without being arrogant.

What do you consider to be your strengths? Your weaknesses?   If you have done a thorough self-assessment, you can easily cite as strengths work habits such as organizational skills or the ability to work independently. You should also mention several concrete skills that relate directly to the job.

Weaknesses are a bit trickier to deal with. Don't deny having weaknesses. Think in advance of a weak point that is not integral to the job. For example, "I need to work on my keyboarding speed," would be a fine response if you were seeking a position in education. Many of us could safely respond that we are always trying to learn new software programs. Be sure to follow up with an explanation of how you are working to correct the problem you've cited. Finally, some people can honestly cite weaknesses that aren't very negative at all. "I tend to take on too much," or "I can be a perfectionist" are examples of this type of "weakness."

Why did you leave your most recent job?   Many people struggle with explanations of why they've left past positions. Remain tactful and diplomatic, but be honest. Never speak negatively about a former employer, but instead explain career moves in terms of your overall skills or plans. For example, you might respond, "My former employer and I decided that the position was not a good match for my skills," or "The position turned out to be incompatible with my new career goals." Of course, if a life event such as a move, birth of a child, or enrollment in college caused you to leave a job, it is perfectly acceptable to say so.

Discuss five major accomplishments.   The trick to responding to this question is remembering that you are the one who can interpret the word *accomplishment*. Few of us can list conquering Mount Everest as an achievement, but many of us have overcome barriers such as limited knowledge or experience. Think of small but meaningful achievements: overcoming shyness with the help of a public speaking course, completing a particularly difficult project, participating in a civic organization that linked you to your college or community, or mastering a new skill.

What questions do you have for me?   Surprisingly, one wrong answer to this question is, "None." It is also a bad idea to ask about salary, benefits, or vacation time at this stage of the interview process. Rather, employers want to know that you are curious and thoughtful and have a good sense of the position for which you are applying. No matter how thorough your research, there is always more to learn about the company and the job. Look over the Questions to Ask an Interviewer section later in this chapter, and don't miss the opportunity this question affords you.

EXERCISE

Identifying Your Interests

As several of the sample questions listed earlier indicate, it is common for employers to ask how you spend your spare time. Although this information may not seem directly relevant to a particular job, it can give the employer additional insight into your personality and your preferences.

Take time to identify your interests before going to an interview. In the spaces below, list the five interests or hobbies you pursue most frequently, and briefly describe your participation. Your answers may range from sports activities to volunteer work to club memberships. In an interview, it may be best to avoid mentioning any political or religious affiliations that could count against you. Use your best judgment in making that decision.

Your Interests

1. _____

    _____

2. _____

    _____

3. _____

    _____

4. _____

    _____

5. _____

    _____

Illegal Interview Questions

There are some things an interviewer shouldn't ask, usually information of a personal nature; it is not uncommon to be asked an illegal question, however. Usually, interviewers ask these questions not out of malice but out of simple ignorance of the law. Although laws vary from state to state, in general interviewers should not ask questions or make comments about your sex, marital status, race, color, religion, housing, physical data, or disabilities.

A smart job hunter is aware of the questions that he is not obligated to answer and knows his options when responding. You have three choices when confronted with an illegal question:

1. Answer the question and ignore the fact that it is not legal.

2. Ask, "I wonder why you would ask that question?" Then, upon hearing the interviewer's response, decide whether or not to answer.

3. Contact the nearest Equal Employment Office. Be aware, however, that although you may have a legitimate claim, it is difficult to prove you have been the victim of discrimination. Hence, this may not be your best option.

Whichever option you choose, consider whether you'd like to work for an employer who is so interested in your personal life. (After you are hired, of course, your company may need personal information, such as your marital status and the names and ages of your children for insurance purposes.)

Seemingly illegal questions are legitimate if they are related to genuine job requirements. For example, it is perfectly acceptable for a shipping company to inquire into your physical stature if your job would require heavy lifting. It would also be appropriate for a company to ask your age if the position required the handling of liquor.

Questions to Ask an Interviewer

Remember that you are interviewing prospective employers at the same time that they are interviewing you. Ask questions that will help you determine whether the position is a good fit for your skills, desires, and career goals. Asking intelligent questions makes you appear interested and enthusiastic. Here are some suggested questions:

1. Tell me about the nature of the position. What are the specific duties and responsibilities? Is a written job description available?

2. What type of training can I expect in the first six months? Down the road?

3. Are there any travel requirements?

4. To whom would I report? Can you tell me something about his or her background?

5. Is this a newly created position? If not, who was the last person to occupy this position, and what is he or she doing now?

6. Does this organization encourage professional growth activities such as participation in business societies or seminars?

7. How long has the company been in business? Tell me about the company's history.

8. What types of customers does the company service? What types of products does it sell?

9. What are the company's plans for the future?

10. What are the future prospects for promotion within the company?

11. Can I provide you with any other information about myself?

12. What is the next step in the decision process? When will a final decision be made regarding the position?

It's best not to inquire about salary during the first interview. With careful research, you should have an idea of the salary range of like positions. In addition, you want to demonstrate that you are more interested in the company and the position than in the money, so delay your questions about salary, benefits, and perks until the second interview or until the company makes you a job offer.

You've Got Personality

Despite the formality of the interview process, the hidden agenda for most interviewers is to get to know you. Although your education and skills are the major deciding factors, it is also important to employers that your personality be a good fit for the job and the company. Don't be afraid to let your personality shine through.

To determine your "personality type," the interviewer searches for personal profile keys in your answers to her questions. Below are some of the personality traits interviewers most often look for.

Personal Profile Keys

- **Drive.** People who are goal oriented are always striving to do better. They like to get tasks accomplished.

- **Motivation.** Enthusiasm and energy go a long way toward success. Employers recognize that a motivated person accepts challenges and is willing to give that little bit extra on the job.

- **Communication skills.** Whatever the company or type of business, the ability to communicate effectively both orally and in writing is vital.

- **Chemistry.** As in personal settings, getting along with others at work is extremely important. Employers appreciate team players, confident individuals, and generally happy people.

- **Energy.** Energetic people get the job done and help motivate those around them. They can be a very positive influence in the work environment.

- **Determination.** Employers want someone who will carry through and finish a project, solve problems, and take on challenges.

- **Confidence.** A confident employee is proud of his accomplishments without being arrogant. Confident people are often very effective in doing their job.

Professional Profile Keys

- **Reliability.** Managers want to be sure they can count on you to get the job done, no matter how challenging it is. In the real world, only performance counts.

- **Honesty.** Employers want someone who is trustworthy and has personal integrity.

- **Pride.** People who take pride in their work always do a good job. They pay attention to details and seek to do things "right," not just "good enough."

- **Dedication.** The best employees are those who make the effort to see a task through to completion. Their commitment to the job makes them valuable assets.

- **Analytical skills.** A person who is able to evaluate a situation, troubleshoot a problem, and take appropriate action makes a good employee.

- **Listening skills.** People who listen show they care. They value others' opinions and learn from those around them. They are also good at following directions.

Achievement Profile Keys

- **Ability to save money.** Every company seeks to minimize its expenses.

- **Ability to save time.** Your productivity ultimately saves the company money. Someone who can follow procedures or recommend improvements to existing procedures enhances the company's organization and, ultimately, its profitability.

- **Ability to earn money.** If you can contribute to the bottom line, any company will consider you an asset.

Employers' Most Wanted List

Employers are searching for candidates with a few highly desirable traits. Among them:

1. Attention to detail	98%
2. Reading skills	95%
3. Ability to cooperate with people	94%
4. Willingness to make an extra effort to increase quality of performance	92%
5. Ability to work under pressure	91%
6. Verbal and communication skills	90%
7. Ability to manage time, be productive	89%
8. Ability to adapt, be flexible	89%
9. Ability to solve problems	84%
10. Ability to interpret and integrate information	83%
11. Ability to set priorities	82%
12. Good grooming and personal hygiene	79%
13. Writing skills	79%
14. Math skills	74%

Source: Career Source, 1997–98 edition

EXERCISE   Go through the lists of profile keys and check the ones you think apply to you. Then select one trait from each of the keys—Personal, Professional, and Achievement—and briefly write about a situation in which you demonstrated that trait, whether at school, at home, or on the job. You should end up with a total of three different stories.

Example: From the list of Professional Profile Keys, *dedication:* Once when a co-worker called in sick, I worked a double shift to complete an important project within the deadline.

Once you have identified specific situations in which you applied these positive traits, you'll be prepared to share these anecdotes with an interviewer should the appropriate opportunity present itself.

Mind Your Body Language

When you interview for a job, it's important to make the best possible impression. To do so, you should monitor not only *what* you say, but *how* you say it. Did you know that people show 55 percent of their feelings and emotions nonverbally? Thirty-eight percent of a message is carried by tone of voice. Only 7 percent of your feelings and emotions are conveyed by the actual words you use.

Your "silent" message is conveyed through signals in your body language. Positive signals can indicate agreement, openness, acceptance, and interest. Negative signals can reveal disagreement, suspicion, rejection, and defensiveness. Become attuned to the nonverbal signals you give off, and watch others' body language, to determine their receptiveness to you.

Positive Signals	*Negative Signals*
Good eye contact	Poor eye contact
Leaning forward	Slumping or turning away
Uncrossing arms or legs	Crossing arms or legs
Nodding head in approval	Shaking head in disapproval
Smiling, occasional laughing	No response
Unbuttoning jacket	Buttoning jacket
Rapt attention	Doodling or blank stare
Palms or wrists turned outward, open	Hands in pockets
Raised eyebrows	Narrowed eyes, sideways glances
Steepling fingers	Making a fist

In an interview, it is helpful to monitor not only your own, but also the interviewer's, body language for instant feedback on how you're doing. If you receive positive signals while discussing a certain area, continue discussion in the same vein. If you detect negative signals, try to modify your approach. You may find, too, that the interviewer begins to imitate your signals. For example, when you

When meeting a prospective employer for an interview, be sure to make good eye contact and give a firm, confident hand-shake. (© Jim Cummins/ Getty Images)

lean forward, the interviewer may do the same. This copying of signals usually indicates agreement, and you may even encourage a good reaction from the interviewer by subtly copying his signals.

As you observe and interpret body language, remember that each separate signal may not be a definitive indicator of a person's emotions. People have their own mannerisms or habits, so it is most meaningful to evaluate clusters or groups of signals to decipher the true message.

After the Interview: Follow Up

The interview is over. Now is the time to assess your performance so that every interview, good or bad, can be a learning experience. Determine what you did right and what aspects you could improve upon. Put in writing some suggestions for your next interview. Be sure to conduct your self-evaluation within a day of the interview; otherwise you're apt to forget portions of the conversation.

EXERCISE

Interview Self-Evaluation

Photocopy this interview self-evaluation form for future use. Then complete the following statements about your last interview.

1. I would describe my initial greeting with the interviewer as _____

    _____

2. I was good at _____

3. I would improve _____

4. My appearance was _____

5. The next time I dress for an interview, I'll _____

    _____

6. I was   ❑ on time   ❑ late   ❑ early

7. When I spoke during the interview, my voice was _____

    _____

8. My body language and eye contact during the interview could be described as

    _____

9. The interviewer was more interested in   ❑ talking   ❑ listening

    I adjusted my interview style accordingly by _____

10. I conveyed the following points about my skills: _____

    _____

11. The toughest question I faced was _____

    I handled this question _____

    The next time I'm asked that question, I'll _____

12. My overall mood and degree of relaxation was _____

    _____

13. Here is a list of things I need to do next to land this job:

    a. Thank-you letters _____

    b. Follow-up phone calls _____

    c. Other _____

    _____

    _____

14 Hill Street
Middletown, KY 83103
March 3, 2003

Mr. Michael Quinn
President, Technopro, Inc.
672 Charles Avenue
Bedford, KY 83102

Dear Mr. Quinn:

Thank you for taking the time to meet with me on Monday. I enjoyed touring Technopro and learning more about your business.

As I mentioned in the interview, I would be very interested in the bookkeeper position and feel I could be an asset to Technopro. Thank you for your consideration. I look forward to hearing from you soon.

Sincerely,

Lindsay Dorsett

Lindsay Dorsett

Sample 12.1: Thank-You Letter to Follow Up Immediately after Interview (may be typed or handwritten)

Career-Search Organization Chart

Remember, looking for a job is your full-time job. Use the chart below to organize your search. Add dates to the chart as you complete each step. Before beginning, photocopy this chart for future use.

Prospective Employer, Contact Person, Title, Address/Phone	Research Completed	Date Inquiry Letter Sent	Date Cover Letter/ Résumé Sent	Date of Follow-Up Phone Call	Interview Date/Time	Thank-You Note Sent	Remarks

Nontraditional Ways to Get an Interview

Occasionally, the job hunter needs to try something unique to get a foot in the door. Although networking, telephone calls, and letters are the traditional approaches to securing an interview, you may reach the point where you're ready to become more creative and aggressive.

A WARNING: Not all employers endorse these approaches. Consider how conservative your career field is, what traditional methods you haven't yet tried, and what you have to lose. Remember, too, that some career experts swear that unorthodox approaches are the best. Use your best judgment, and when you've carefully considered your options, make a plan.

1. Send your résumé to the person you'd like to work for via an express mail service or courier marked "Personal and Confidential."

2. Get creative with your résumé. Make it very large or very small, make a puzzle out of it, or print it on neon orange paper. In your cover letter, explain your unusual presentation. For example, you might start out, "I'm the piece of the puzzle Brown, Incorporated, has been looking for." Accompany a tiny résumé with a letter that begins, "Sometimes it's easy to overlook the obvious choice."

3. Send a videotaped résumé.

4. Create a business card giving your name, phone number, and a few of your best qualifications. When you meet potential contacts, give them your card.

5. Put a position wanted ad in the newspaper.

6. Learn whether the prospective employer belongs to any local clubs or organizations. Go to a meeting to network and introduce yourself.

7. Send a clever e-mail to your prospect.

8. Send a series of postcards. The first might read, "Wish I was there." Send more information on each one.

9. Learn what the employer's hobby is. Send an appropriate item. For example, you might send an avid sailor a model sailboat. You may need to enlist the aid of a secretary to find out this information. These small gifts might be most appropriate after the interview.

10. Send an object related to your name. Reginald King might send a crown; Dawn Greenleaf might send a pressed four-leaf clover.

11. Send a photograph with your résumé printed on the reverse.

12. Send an unusual object with an explanation. For example, send some shoelaces with a note that reads, "I'm sorry you've been tied up, but I'm hoping we can get off on the right foot." Send a jar of cinnamon with a few words about how you can add spice to the company.

EXERCISE

Brainstorm two or three other nontraditional methods to obtain an interview that might be suitable for your career field or position. Write them here.

1. _____

_____

2. _____

_____

3. _____

_____

4. _____

_____

5. _____

_____

When you've committed yourself to one of these guerrilla tactics, carry it off with confidence and enthusiasm. It may turn out to be the most profitable and memorable of your job-hunting experiences.

Reasons for Unsuccessful Interviews

Job applicants are frequently rejected because of the following behaviors or characteristics that become apparent during interviews:

1. Too interested in starting salary
2. Uncertainty about job/career or long-range goals
3. Poor personal appearance
4. Overbearing, overaggressive, conceited, or "know-it-all" behavior
5. Inability to express self clearly—poor voice, diction, grammar
6. Lack of interest and enthusiasm—passive, indifferent
7. Lack of confidence and poise—nervous, ill at ease
8. Poor scholastic record—just got by
9. Unwilling to start at the bottom—expects too much too soon
10. Makes excuses—evasive, hedges on unfavorable factors in record

11. Lack of tact

12. Condemnation of past employers

13. Lack of maturity

14. Lack of courtesy—ill-mannered

15. Marked dislike for schoolwork

16. Lack of vitality

17. Fails to look interviewer in the eye

18. Limp, fishlike handshake

19. Loafs during vacations

20. Unhappy married life

21. Friction with parents

22. Sloppy application form

23. Merely shopping around

24. Wants job only for a short time

25. Little sense of humor

26. No interest in company or industry

27. Lack of knowledge in field of specialization

28. Parents make all major decisions

29. Emphasis on whom she knows

30. Cynical

31. Lazy

32. Intolerant—strong prejudices

33. Narrow interests

34. Inability to take criticism

35. Lack of appreciation of the value of experience

36. Radical ideas

37. Late to interview without good reason

38. Knows nothing about company

39. Fails to express appreciation for interviewer's time

40. Asks no questions about the job

EXERCISE   See if you can come up with a few reasons of your own that someone might "fail" an interview.

1. _____

2. _____

3. _____

Select three inappropriate interview behaviors or characteristics from the list on pages 190–191 or from your own responses, and brainstorm ways to remedy these negatives. For example, if you select item 16, lack of vitality, you might think of extending a firm handshake and giving an enthusiastic greeting as ways to convey your energy and vitality to an interviewer.

Handling Rejection

Nobody likes rejection, but it happens to everyone at some time in his career. Remember that fact as you seek employment. Many people spend months searching and interviewing for dozens of jobs before they receive an appealing offer. When the economy is depressed, months can turn into years before the right position turns up. So don't get discouraged if you don't achieve instant success.

When you're first making the rounds, try not to be personally offended if potential employers don't return your calls. Realize that they may be busy and that your call represents an interruption, and certainly not a priority, in their day.

What You Don't Know

Try not to take it personally if you are not offered a job after having what you consider a successful interview. You may feel that you are perfectly suited to a particular position, but the employer may not. There may be other candidates who have more experience, skills that more precisely match the job's responsibilities, or a personality more compatible with management practices.

You may be rejected for reasons that have absolutely nothing to do with you. For instance, there may be an in-house candidate that has a leg up on the job, but nonetheless company policy dictates that outside candidates must be interviewed. Or perhaps a current employee has a personal connection to one of the other candidates.

Sometimes it's a salary issue—the employer knows you're the best candidate but nonetheless settles for a lower-salaried, less-qualified individual. Or you may be overqualified, leading the employer to conjecture that you won't want to stay in the position long-term but are using it as a steppingstone to a job at your level.

Most likely, you'll never be privy to the real reason you weren't selected. Employers are careful not to divulge any hiring information that could result in a lawsuit. The important thing is to look upon every rejection as a learning experience. Make your most educated guess as to why the outcome was not what you wanted. Look for specific ways to improve your presentation.

Finally, remember that finding a job is a numbers game: The more people you contact and the more interviews you have, the more likely you are to land a job.

The Right Frame of Mind

Rare is the individual who begins job hunting and is immediately offered the quintessential dream job. Most job hunts take time and effort. You'll be better equipped to handle a challenging job search if you maintain a positive attitude. Keep these tips in mind:

1. **Believe in yourself.** You've worked hard to get where you are today. You've acquired the skills you need. Now it's just a matter of time until you find an opportunity to put them to use. Dare to dream. Pursue ideas and opportunities that are of interest and value to you. Exude confidence in all you do.

2. **Look at the big picture.** Don't let the little things get you down. Learn from your mistakes. Keep your perspective and focus on what's important.

3. **Don't feel angry or bitter.** It's easy to be upset when employers don't recognize the wonderful asset you could be to their companies, but don't internalize the rejection. Besides being self-destructive, your anger will come through in future interviews.

4. **Be creative.** Don't give up. Find unique solutions to problems. Keep generating new ideas. Think beyond the traditional answers. Look for a market niche, and develop a creative way to fill that niche.

5. **Be flexible.** Plan your job search, but reevaluate and change your plan as you learn new things and meet new people. Expect the unexpected. Develop contingency plans to handle different situations.

6. **Be optimistic.** Focus on the positive aspects of all occurrences—even negative ones. If one approach fails, be prepared to try another.

7. **Don't be afraid to take risks.** Accept the fact that finding, and eventually accepting, a new job involves an element of risk. Learn to manage the risks by identifying them and then limiting their downsides.

8. **Be persistent.** Keep your attention focused on the task at hand. Don't give up until you've found an avenue to success. Keep exploring solutions until you find one that works.

9. **Adopt an action orientation.** Be a doer. Be a decision maker. Take control of a situation and propel yourself toward success.

10. **Have a "plan B."** If your career path is not a smooth one, perhaps it's time to reassess your strategy and goals.

Ask for What You Want

Some job hunters make the mistake of forgetting to ask for what they want. Either because they are too timid or because they assume the employer knows their intentions, they find themselves unpleasantly surprised and disappointed during different phases of their job hunt.

At each step of the search, keep your goal in mind and be sure to clearly communicate it to the appropriate people.

When researching, don't just wander around the library waiting for the appropriate field to present itself. Work up a few topic areas with which to start. Ask the librarian for the kind of help you need—for example, where to find articles on manufacturing or where to find phone books for Denver.

In your cover letter, remember to ask for an interview. Also, specify what you plan to do next, that is, follow up with a phone call or a visit. Don't wait for the employer to call you. Follow up each letter promptly.

In an interview, close by asking for the job (assuming that you still want it). Tell interviewers that it's been a pleasure meeting them and that you'd enjoy working with them. Make it clear that you want the position. Be enthusiastic and positive. In your thank-you notes and in all other follow-up letters, state that you are well suited to the responsibilities and challenges of the position.

At each phase of your job hunt, a small goal should be clear in your mind. Sometimes, stating these goals aloud or writing them down can help you achieve them.

A Final Note on Follow Up

It bears repeating that the thank-you note is a good indicator of a job hunter's follow-through, etiquette, and attention to detail. This small gesture has a big impact and should be considered essential after every interview. Few job hunters remember this important step. Those who do stand out; they also succeed in putting their names in front of the employer one more time while creating good will and a lasting, positive impression.

If you haven't heard anything after an interview and think it's time to reconnect with the employer, feel free to write a quick note or e-mail or pick up the phone. Here are some suggestions for things you might say:

> "I'm still very interested in the position. Are there any questions I can answer or anything I can do to make this work for you?"

> "I was thinking about what you said regarding the _____ project, and I have some ideas that I think could help. See attached."

> "I've been offered a job with another company. However, your firm would be my first choice. I wanted to check with you on the status of the position we discussed before I accept this other offer."

> "I enjoyed our conversation about _____ . I happened to see an article on the subject in _____ (insert publication name) and thought you might be interested in it. See enclosed."

Passing the Test

Learning Objectives

In this chapter, you will learn about the methods used by today's employers to protect themselves in hiring new employees. Among them are:

- Drug tests
- Skills tests
- Psychological or personality tests
- Physicals
- Background checks
- Probation periods

Chapter 13

STRATEGIES in ACTION

Oksana desperately wanted the position of manager of convention services for a high-end resort located in Las Vegas. She had already survived three lengthy interviews and was told she was the lead candidate. All that remained was for her to take a personality test. Oksana was confident she would ace that test as she did most written exams. What she didn't realize, however, was that the test was not one that would be graded. Rather, for the employer it was a means of gaining insight into Oksana's personality. The employer was specifically seeking someone who could work well on a team and serve as a leader who motivated coworkers and encouraged them to take on increasingly challenging responsibilities.

Unfortunately, Oksana's background was about to work against her. She'd run her own travel agency for many years and had made all her own decisions. A strong individualist, she was used to working alone and taking control of all situations.

Those traits quickly became obvious on Oksana's personality test. Although Oksana had all the experience and knowledge needed to do well in the convention services position, she clearly lacked the teamworking skills that the employer viewed as a necessity.

Ultimately, the employer decided to hire another candidate. Oksana was initially upset to have lost what she viewed as the perfect job, but she had to admit that the personality profile had been accurate. Most likely, she would not have been successful or happy in the position. Rather than regarding the experience as a failure, Oksana chose to use the information she now had about her psychological makeup and work style to find a job that was better suited to her personality.

Employment Tests

Because hiring the right employees is so critical to a company's success, many employers require their leading candidates to take tests. Drug testing is becoming more widespread each year. Proficiency or competency tests that measure an applicant's abilities in a specific area are also common. Medical exams are used to check an applicant's overall health and physical ability to do a job. For professional positions, psychological or personality tests have gained popularity as a means of helping employers correctly match candidates with the responsibilities of a position.

Your prospective employer will tell you which tests are required and will give you instructions for taking them.

Drug Tests

An increasing number of employers require preemployment blood or urine tests, to avoid the problems a drug user can bring to the job. These tests reveal the presence of cocaine, marijuana, opiates, amphetamines, and barbiturates.

Although some employers provide assistance and counseling to current workers who develop drug problems, they are unlikely to take on a new worker who shows signs of drug abuse. Their reasoning is sound: Drug abuse is likely to cost the company in terms of increased absenteeism, increased chances of on-the-job mistakes or accidents, and potential embarrassment should customers learn of the problem. In addition, alcohol and drug abuse may raise the company's health insurance costs.

Current estimates reveal that nearly 60 percent of employers test college recruits for drug use. That figure is likely to rise in future years as more employers become aware of the difficulties associated with workers who have substance-abuse problems.

Skills Tests

Depending on the type of job you apply for, you may be asked to take tests that measure specific abilities. Some examples:

- A data entry clerk might take a typing test.

- A secretary might take typing, spelling, and computer-skills tests.

- A telemarketer might take a speech/voice test.

- A bookkeeper might take a math-skills test.

- A reporter might take a writing-skills test.

- A dancer might have to audition.

Usually, you can't cram for this type of exam, but you can put your mind at ease by knowing what to expect. Find out all you can about the test beforehand. Try to relax, so that your true skills will be apparent. Also, as you're taking the test, remember that it is probably not the deciding factor in whether you are hired. It is just a way for an employer to get a more complete picture of your capabilities.

Psychological or Personality Tests

There is increasing recognition that interpersonal style is just as important to success as technical skills, and that psychological tests are therefore helpful recruitment tools for certain professional jobs. According to a *Wall Street Journal* report, approximately 40 percent of Fortune 500 companies today require job candidates to take a psychological test—double the 1999 rate.

Unlike most tests you've probably encountered, this is not a pass-or-fail type of exam with right or wrong answers. Rather, it's a test to determine such things as your personality type, your ability to get along with others, how you handle stress, whether you're honest, and the amount of energy you'll bring to the job. It may also be used to identify the kind of position in which you would be most successful.

In 1989, Congress banned most private-sector applications of the polygraph test, voice stress analysis, and other electronic screening methods. Many private employers who previously depended on these tests have turned to psychological testing to help them select the best job applicants.

Psychological tests usually consist of about fifty multiple-choice questions. Sometimes tests are "graded" in house; in other cases, they are sent for evaluation to the firm that created the test. Results may appear in the form of a description of the applicant's personality or may simply state whether the applicant is recommended for hire or should be considered with caution.

The key to success on a psychological test is to answer the questions with regard to yourself in the context of the professional position for which you are applying. Don't answer the questions from the point of view of your personal life—unless your professional and personal personas are identical. That is, don't lie or compromise your personal integrity, but be aware that as a student or working professional, you've learned a set of behavioral patterns that enable you to be successful and productive. It is those behavioral patterns that determine whether you will make a good hire. Take the psychological test with these two strategies in mind:

1. As you answer each question, think to yourself: How has my experience as a student or working person taught me to think and respond to this? Use your learned professional behavior traits to select the correct answer.

2. Look at yourself from the employer's point of view. Determine which traits enable you to handle your responsibilities effectively. Those are the traits you want to call attention to in your psychological test.

Most likely, there will be no imposed time limit when you take the test, so make sure to consider each question carefully. Be aware that the test may contain "double blinds," in which you are asked a question early in the test and then asked almost the same question worded slightly differently later in the test. This technique is based on the belief that most of us can tell a lie but few of us can remember that lie under stress. So if we are dishonest in answering a question, we may answer the same question differently later.

You are likely to encounter such ethics questions as, "Have you ever stolen anything?" or "Have you ever told a lie?" The goal of the employer is to determine if you will be an honest employee.

Don't seek to project a false image of yourself through the answers you select. Employers are simply looking for people who will fit into their corporate culture and who have well-adjusted personal and professional lives.

Unfortunately, you may never find out exactly how you did on the test or what it revealed about your personality. Employers are not obligated to give you the results, and many are fearful of saying something that could expose them to a discrimination lawsuit. If you get the job, you'll know you did fine. If not, don't assume you "failed" the psychological test. As you know by now, job applicants are selected or not selected for a myriad of reasons. Learn from the experience, and move on to your next job-hunting adventure.

Physicals

You may be asked to have a medical exam as a condition of employment. In some cases, you'll be able to see your own doctor. In others, you will be asked to see a physician contracted by the employer.

A medical exam is allowable only after an offer has been extended and only if it is job related and required of all new employees in the same job category. The job offer may be contingent on the successful outcome of the exam.

Physical agility tests are not considered medical exams and may be given at any point in the application or employment process. Tests must be job related and administered to all applicants or employees in a job category.

There are two reasons for medical exams and physical agility tests: to evaluate your physical health before the job begins, and to ensure that your physical capabilities—with or without accommodation—will meet the demands of the job.

Background Checks

After the terrorist attacks on September 11, 2001, many employers began scrutinizing the histories of job applicants in an effort to protect their personnel and facilities from an attack within. One of the most common tacks is running a criminal background check to see if the applicant has an arrest record. Numerous employers have, in the last few years, implemented stricter hiring policies that summarily eliminate candidates with any type of prior criminal offense.

Employers may also check an applicant's credit history to look for debt problems or bankruptcy filings. They believe that how you run your personal life gives clues about how you will operate in your professional life. Although it may seem a violation of privacy, the business climate today is one of erring on the side of caution.

Finally, many employers routinely run résumé checks; that is, they verify facts such as your educational degrees, professional licenses, achievements, and previous employment and salaries. They are searching for exaggeration, misleading information, or outright lies that reflect a dishonest or unethical candidate.

Probation Periods

Because of the cost of hiring and training new employees, employers are likely to take every possible precaution to ensure candidates will work out before making long-term commitments to them. For that reason, employers may insist on a probation period for new hires. This period, lasting usually from one to three months, gives the employer an opportunity to evaluate your skills and see if your personality is a match for the company. It is typical that during the trial period, employees are not given any benefits or health insurance coverage.

If an employer says you must go through a probation period, don't take it personally. Most likely it is standard operating procedure. You should be sure to find out what the terms of your employment will be after probation, however. Clarify such items as the following:

- Salary

- Health insurance

- Other benefits

- Vacation time, that is, does your probation period count toward earned vacation time?

- Salary review. If the terms of your hire state you will be reviewed in one year, clarify whether that year includes the time served while on probation.

Part Four

GETTING TO WORK

Evaluating Job Offers

Learning Objectives

In this chapter, you will learn to do the following:

- Evaluate a job offer
- Negotiate your salary
- Write a job acceptance letter
- Write a job rejection letter

Chapter 14

STRATEGIES
in ACTION

Pablo held two job offers in his hand. After months of job hunting and numerous interviews, two companies were interested in hiring him. Now it was up to Pablo to decide which position to accept.

The first offer was from a large, multinational company. Pablo knew that if he joined this company, he would be initiated with a formal orientation program and be given specific responsibilities appropriate for his entry-level status. The potential for growth was relatively good, because the company was expanding rapidly. Excellent benefits and a good starting salary made the offer very attractive.

The second position was with a small, established business. With this company, Pablo's responsibilities would be much broader. He'd have to wear many different hats. The owner made it clear that Pablo would be integrally involved in all major projects and might be required to do tasks that were a stretch for his current skill level. Because there was no formal training program, Pablo would have to learn on the job. He would receive a basic benefits package and a starting annual salary several thousand dollars below that offered by the first company.

Pablo began to write down the pros and cons of each position. He decided to put the money issue aside and focus instead on which job would better fit his personality, abilities, and long-term career objectives. Because this was his first job in the field, he felt it might serve as the steppingstone for all his future endeavors.

After much consideration, Pablo chose the smaller company. He liked that he would play a key role in all major projects and would be challenged with many new responsibilities. Pablo knew he was a fast learner and would catch on quickly, even without formal training. He thought the smaller company offered him the chance to quickly gain lots of experience in diverse areas in his field. Even though the salary would be lower, Pablo believed that the experience and knowledge he would gain would in the long run enable him to progress to more responsible positions in his field with higher salaries.

Choose the Best Job for You

Congratulations! Your hard work and professionalism have resulted in several job offers. Now you are faced with a decision that many people would envy.

EXERCISE

To help choose the job that is right for you, complete the following exercise step by step. The process may be time consuming, but good decisions require careful consideration.

Step 1. The chart below will help you evaluate your career options. It lists a number of job variables; fill in the blank spaces at the bottom of the left-hand column with other factors that are important to you in weighing one position against another.

		Job Option 1: _____	*Job Option 2:* _____	*Job Option 3:* _____
Rank	*Job Variables*	*Company Name*	*Company Name*	*Company Name*
_____	Benefits	_____	_____	_____
_____	Service to others	_____	_____	_____
_____	Challenge	_____	_____	_____
_____	Creativity	_____	_____	_____
_____	Schedule	_____	_____	_____
_____	Status	_____	_____	_____
_____	Title	_____	_____	_____
_____	Responsibilities	_____	_____	_____
_____	Satisfaction	_____	_____	_____
_____	Salary	_____	_____	_____
_____	Acceptable commute	_____	_____	_____
_____	Good work environment	_____	_____	_____
_____	Appropriate training	_____	_____	_____
_____	Educational opportunities	_____	_____	_____
_____	Acceptable supervisor	_____	_____	_____
_____	Possibility for promotion	_____	_____	_____
_____	Flexibility	_____	_____	_____
_____	_____	_____	_____	_____
_____	_____	_____	_____	_____
_____	_____	_____	_____	_____
_____	_____	_____	_____	_____
_____	_____	_____	_____	_____

Step 2. Now rank each job variable according to its importance to you. Careful, honest self-evaluation will help you decide which aspects of employment you value most. Would you endure a long commute to earn a higher salary? Do you need a company that provides in-house child care? Is being able to work outdoors extremely important to you? You might have added these factors to the bottom of the variable list. If you decide that a factor is unimportant to you, rank it last or cross it off the list.

Step 3. Circle your top five variables.

Step 4. Open your mind to any feasible options to which you haven't yet given full consideration. Returning to school, traveling, joining the military, or returning to a former position are examples of such options; don't rule out any of them yet. If you think of options other than the immediate job offers, create columns for them.

Step 5. Examine each job variable in light of each job option. Go to the blank under Job Option 1 and across from your number one job variable. Mark the blank with a check, a check plus, or a check minus, indicating whether the job meets your needs, exceeds your expectations, or falls short of your requirements. Examine every job variable under Job Option 1 in this way. Do the same for the other job options. You may discover you aren't sure how a particular employment offer meets your requirements with regard to one of the variables. Mark that blank with a question mark and be sure to include the relevant variable on a list of questions to ask your contact person later (see the fill-in items below).

Job Option 1   **Questions to ask** _____ **(contact person)**

  1. _____

  2. _____

  3. _____

Job Option 2   **Questions to ask** _____ **(contact person)**

  1. _____

  2. _____

  3. _____

Job Option 3   **Questions to ask** _____ **(contact person)**

  1. _____

  2. _____

  3. _____

Step 6. Now you have carefully considered what is important to you in your career and you've also examined all your job options. Look carefully down the column under each option. Which column has the most check pluses for your top five priorities? This is probably the option to choose.

Before discussing salary with a potential employer, be sure you've done your homework. You should know the typical pay scale for the job you're seeking. With an amount in mind, you're more likely to be successful in your negotiations.
(© Stephen Derr/Getty Images)

Negotiate Your Salary

Discuss salary with your prospective employer only after all other items have been firmed up, because this is likely to be the biggest negotiating point. Also, you don't want to give the impression that you consider salary to be the most important aspect of your employment; rather, you want the employer to believe you are genuinely interested in the job and its responsibilities. However, don't ever accept a job without knowing the salary. In fact, you should go into an interview knowing how much you want to make, and work toward that goal.

Before you discuss salary requirements with your potential employer:

1. Research the typical salary range for the position you're considering, including the geographical consideration of what this type of position pays in your area. There are several ways to do this. Trade journals often do salary surveys for their industry; check the library for the current year's issue. Call trade associations. Ask others in the field. Read classified ads, which often list salaries along with job requirements. Search the Internet.

   Many major career sites list salary data. This information is particularly useful if you're considering relocating, because it enables you to compare the

Humorous Negotiations

Reaching the end of a job interview, the human resources representative asked the young engineer fresh out of college, "And what starting salary were you looking for?"

The engineer said, "In the neighborhood of $150,000 a year, depending on the benefits package."

The human resources representative said, "Well, what would you say to a package of 5 weeks vacation, 14 paid holidays, full medical and dental insurance, company-matching retirement fund to 50% of salary, and a company car leased every two years, say, a red Corvette?"

The engineer sat up straight and said, "Wow! Are you kidding?"

The human resources representative said, "Certainly . . . but you started it."

Source: www.jokemaster.com

salary for a specific position in your current location with that in the area you may move to.

2. Try to find out how much the person who held the job before you was paid.

3. Decide how important salary is to you at this stage in your career. Does this job represent a good steppingstone or entrée into the company?

4. Remember that some jobs have flexible salaries and some do not. Try to ascertain into which category your position falls. Jobs requiring more advanced skills usually have more pay flexibility, because people's varied experience and credentials have to be taken into consideration.

5. Consider the health of the local economy. If the economy is weak, you'll have less negotiating power. If the economy is strong, you'll be able to exercise more clout.

6. Assess the demand for your skills. If they are highly specialized, you may have an edge in negotiation. If they are more general and are shared with numerous other applicants, you may not.

During salary negotiation:

1. Let the employer say the first number. Realize that this initial offer is most likely below what the company is actually willing to pay.

2. If you must state a figure, give a range you would consider. Aim high, but be realistic. Researchers have found a strong correlation between people's aspirations and the results they achieve in negotiation. Observe the employer's body language and overall response to judge whether your range is in the ballpark. Remember, too, that many employers are good actors when it comes to negotiating salaries.

3. Be firm, not wishy-washy, when stating your salary requirements. Say, "I want X" instead of "Well, I know this is probably too much, but I'd like to make X. Is that a problem?"

4. When the employer throws out a number, don't just accept it. Respond with "I was hoping for something closer to X." Make sure that "X" is an amount higher than you think you can actually get. This leaves room for compromise.

5. You can discuss your salary in weekly, monthly, or annual terms, as long as you understand how the numbers add up or break down.

6. Avoid mentioning what you made at your previous job, especially if you are seeking a large hike in pay. If push comes to shove, answer honestly, but explain that your responsibilities in the new position sound like they would be much more challenging.

7. Focus on objective criteria. It will be easier to win the employer's agreement if she sees that your expectations are firmly grounded on objective information, such as what similar firms pay people with like experience.

8. When negotiating, focus on the qualities you bring to the job more than on the salary. You will be most persuasive if you make the employer feel you are worthy of the salary you want.

9. Think about whether you can afford to live on the salary being offered. Be sure to account for state and federal taxes, which will come out of your pay. Remember that the cost of living varies from place to place.

10. Don't be lulled into accepting less now in return for an offer to renegotiate your salary in three to six months when you've proven yourself. When that day comes, you'll have no leverage, having already invested time and energy into your current position.

11. Take into consideration benefits such as health insurance, stock options, retirement investment programs, and vacation time.

12. Find out how big a premium is deducted from your salary for health insurance, as nearly all employers today require at least a minimum contribution from their employees. Evaluate the quality of the health insurance plan. With medical costs skyrocketing, a good insurance plan can be an important benefit.

13. Don't consider Christmas bonuses as part of your salary. You'll receive those bonuses only if the company is doing well and only at the discretion of the employer. In addition, you don't want to have to wait until Christmas to get your money.

14. If commissions are part of your salary, get an indication of realistic expectations. The employer will probably highlight the earnings of people who make the highest commissions while downplaying those of people who earn average or below-average commissions.

15. Ask how often salary reviews are conducted and how large raises tend to be in terms of percentage of overall salary. As with estimates of commissions, the employer may exaggerate this claim.

16. Get promises in writing. ("We'll review your salary in six months," and so on.)

17. Avoid ultimatums, threats, and other coercive behavior. If you reach a critical impasse in the discussion, ask whether you can think about the salary and get back to the employer. This will provide an opportunity for tensions to subside and for you to assess your options.

18. Finally, review your results, whether good or bad. The best way to improve your negotiating ability is to learn from your experiences. After you finish negotiations, reflect on what you did that worked well and what you might want to do differently the next time.

The End Is in Sight

It's time to take a huge breath, give a sigh of relief, and pat yourself on the back. You've come a long way to get to this point—the crossroads where you must decide to either accept or reject an offer. Because you cannot predict the future, be sure you handle this final task with as much professionalism as you did earlier job-hunting activities, such as writing your résumé and interviewing. That is to say, you want the employer to like and respect you regardless of whether you choose to accept the position. Now go ahead and sit down at your keyboard; you've got at least one more letter to write.

The Acceptance Letter

Once you've decided which job you want to take, it's time to wrap things up. The acceptance letter serves several purposes. It is an opportunity to thank the hiring party, to express enthusiasm for the position, and most importantly, to define the terms of your employment as agreed upon in your negotiations. Send letters to every person who was directly involved in the hiring process. (There may come a time down the road when you'll be glad you put this information in writing.) Your acceptance letter should include a statement of the following issues:

- Job title
- Salary
- Contract terms
- Starting date

The Rejection Letter

You may have thought employers were the only ones who get to write rejection letters. Not true. Here's your big chance. If you have decided against accepting a position you've been offered, you should take the time to formally decline in writing. You never know if one day you may be calling that employer again for a job; you want to be remembered positively. Your rejection letter should cover these issues:

- A courteous thank you for the employer's time and consideration
- A brief explanation of why you are not accepting the position
- A statement of any hopes you may have to work with that employer in the future

131 East Robin Street
Milville, Virginia 23331
July 12, 2000

Mr. John Michaels
Medco Ltd.
14 Collie Street
Kingston, Virginia 23332

Dear Mr. Michaels:

I was very pleased to receive your letter of July 5, 2000, offering me the job of secretary for Medco's southern division. The conditions of employment meet my requirements, and I would like to accept the position.

As per our agreement, I will begin work on July 30, 2000, at a starting salary of $25,000. I look forward to working with a company as dynamic and progressive as Medco.

Sincerely,

Mary Carlson

Mary Carlson

Sample 14.1: Letter to Accept a Position

10 Cypress Avenue
Hollywood, CA 91472
May 16, 2000

Ms. Sandra Miles
Marketing Director
Quistron Corp.
17 W. 4th Avenue
Hollywood, CA 91473

Dear Ms. Miles:

After much thought, I have decided not to accept the position in the Marketing Department of Quistron Corp. Although I very much appreciate the offer, I feel the position is not in line with my goals at this stage in my career.

Thank you for taking the time to meet with me and consider my qualifications. Should my situation change, I will certainly contact you.

Cordially,

Janet Massi

Janet Massi

Sample 14.2: Letter to Reject a Position

Learning Your New Job

Chapter 15

Janelle well remembered her first day at work several months ago. The mere thought of it brought back that feeling of butterflies and a painful tightness in her throat. She had literally shook as she rode the elevator to her new office, where she'd be a clothing buyer for a major retailer. It was the very job Janelle had dreamed of, but now, faced with the actual work, everything seemed so difficult. There were hundreds of products, dozens of vendors, and incredibly complex procedures for placing even the smallest order. The list of things she had to learn had seemed endless.

Now, Janelle could look back with pride and appreciate just how far she'd come. She could reel off from memory the sku number of almost every clothing item the store stocked; she knew all the vendors by name and even remembered the names of their spouses and kids; and she could whip through the ordering procedures while simultaneously carrying on detailed conversations with her coworkers about their weekend plans. The job was anything but routine, however. Janelle felt comfortable in her position and proud that she hadn't given up even when everything had seemed so new and overwhelming.

Your First Few Days on the Job

Your first few days on the job are a lot like your first days in a new school—you look forward to a new beginning filled with exciting possibilities, but you're a bundle of nerves. What if they don't like you? What if you say the wrong thing? What if the job isn't what you thought it would be?

It's not surprising that starting a new job is frequently listed as one of the top ten most stressful events in a person's life. Here are some suggestions to help you fit in and succeed:

1. **Write it down.** Bring a pad wherever you go, and jot down important information. You're likely to be overwhelmed with details—everything from where the rest room is to coworkers' names to your specific responsibilities. If you take good notes and review them during downtime, you'll quickly commit the important information to memory.

2. **Just ask.** Don't be afraid of sounding stupid. The quickest way to find out "what's going on" is to ask. Better now than later when you're in the midst of a project with a tight deadline and don't have a clue what to do. Additionally, asking good questions makes you appear interested in your job and intent on doing it right.

3. **Be enthusiastic.** Show eagerness to do the job at hand. You're excited to be in this new position and open to the many opportunities it will present. It doesn't hurt to let some of that natural enthusiasm show through.

4. **Hold your opinions.** Every company has its own way of getting work done. Most likely, the policies and procedures that governed the work flow at a previous job don't apply here. Don't think that you'll change everyone over to your way of thinking. First learn their methods, be flexible, and adapt.

5. **Be optimistic.** Don't get discouraged if you feel overwhelmed. It doesn't matter if you're a secretary or a CEO; everyone experiences a learning curve when starting a new job. The first days are the worst, but rest assured your anxiety will soon diminish. Before you know it, you'll no longer be the new kid in school!

Your First Few Weeks on the Job

The first few weeks on the job are sure to be challenging. If you're like most people, you'll feel a bit unsure of yourself for a while. But don't let your fears take over; it won't take long until you feel at home. Here are some things to keep in mind as you familiarize yourself with your new position:

1. **Do your homework.** There's no reason that you, as a new employee, need to walk in clueless. Through the Internet and other sources of information, it's

When starting a new job, it's important to observe others and quickly learn as much as you can about the company and your individual responsibilities. (© Bob Daemmrich/ Stock Boston)

easy to research companies and industries. During your first few weeks of employment, take it upon yourself to research anything that is new to you.

2. **Learn your company's policies and procedures.** Some companies have a formal orientation program for new employees, whereas others expect you to "learn as you work."

3. **Become aware of the corporate culture.** Be alert to how people communicate (meetings, memos, face to face, voice mail, or e-mail). Note how the company handles its communications with customers and vendors. Observe the unwritten dress code, and be sure your clothes are appropriate. Become aware of how many hours people work. Some companies are strictly 9 to 5, whereas others expect their workers to put in longer days or take short lunch hours. (Be advised that most companies don't pay salaried workers for overtime.) Adapt your style to that of the company.

4. **Don't try too hard.** Nobody expects you to accomplish miracles overnight. Give yourself time to learn the ropes, or you'll risk making serious gaffes. You may also offend people whose support you'll later need.

5. **Send thank-you messages to the people who helped you job-hunt.** Write or type short notes to all the people you contacted when you were unemployed. Tell them about your new job, and thank them for their support. Your efforts will be appreciated and remembered.

6. **Be discreet about your salary.** It's unprofessional to discuss salary. Never ask or tell anyone about pay, for it will inevitably come back to haunt you.

7. **Clarify expectations.** Determine the mission of the company and how your job fits into that mission. Identify immediate priorities that need to be addressed. Talk to your boss to learn what she expects from you.

8. **Identify the winners.** Figure out who the superstars are at your company. That's usually easy to do because they're well-known and respected. Observe the company's movers and shakers, and learn their secrets to success.

Your First Year on the Job

Your first year of employment will probably constitute the best of times as well as the worst. Most likely, it will include both ups and downs, successes and failures. Here are some strategies you can employ to ensure that your initial year represents a solid beginning:

1. **Learn your job.** Become proficient at the responsibilities for which you were hired. Some people concentrate their efforts on getting promoted without focusing on the tasks at hand. For true on-the-job success, you need to do a great job no matter how trivial your tasks might seem to you. Keep in mind that part of your job is to make your boss look good.

2. **Accept that you will make mistakes.** As you learn on the job, you will make your share of fumbles. Don't be too hard on yourself. What's important is how you learn from those mistakes.

3. **Focus on performance and results.** Excuses, even the best ones, are not what bosses remember at review time. Solid, consistent performance is the only thing that really matters. Be conscientious and enthusiastic about your work.

4. **Meet deadlines.** In school, you were probably accustomed to having someone else set deadlines—due dates for papers, final exams, final projects, and so forth. At work, you're often responsible for setting your own deadlines, or at least for recognizing when intermediate tasks need to be completed to meet final deadlines. Set parameters, and then be sure to meet them. Remember, performance is the only thing that counts.

5. **Persistence pays off.** In the beginning, a task may seem hard or overwhelming. Stay with it. Eventually you'll get the hang of it.

6. **Take initiative.** Don't be afraid to assume responsibility. Ask questions if you're unclear on something. Request assistance if you need it. Take on projects that others don't want. Show that you're a team player.

7. **Go the extra mile.** Always do more than what's expected of you, never less. Do it without being asked or expecting recognition for your efforts. Remember—attitude is key.

8. **Use common sense.** Try to figure things out on your own before asking for help. Work on developing your own instincts. Be a good listener and you'll accelerate the learning process.

9. **Pay attention to detail.** Detail-oriented people get the job done right, leaving nothing to fall through the cracks.

10. **Make a good impression.** The tendency is for everyone to watch the new employee. The impression you make during the first year will stick with you and set the course for your career.

11. **Dress appropriately.** Wear clothes and jewelry that demonstrate your professionalism. Practice good personal hygiene.

12. **Earn the respect of your coworkers and superiors.** Begin right away to establish your professional image. Let people know you're serious about your work by being honest, responsible, and ethical. Once you prove yourself, you'll gain acceptance among your peers and be acknowledged as a valued part of the team. Resolve any conflicts in a professional manner.

13. **Hone your communication skills.** Ask questions and listen well. Continually strive to improve your speaking and writing abilities.

14. **Practice proper phone etiquette.** Answer your phone with a professional greeting; a simple "hello" just doesn't cut it in a work environment. You may want to

ask your employer how he would prefer that you answer the phone—different companies and positions within companies may have their own requirements.

Be pleasant no matter how tired or exasperated you may be. Speak slowly and distinctly; do not mumble. When you place a call, be sure to identify yourself and to state your business in a clear manner. The office is not the place for personal calls. If you must make or receive an occasional personal call, keep it short and to the point.

15. **Watch your language.** Profanity and slang have no place in the business world. Learn office jargon and use it when appropriate. Focus on being clear in your communication—both written and verbal. Any type of racial or ethnic slur or a comment that could be perceived as sexual harassment is totally unacceptable. Any deviations from this policy can result in serious legal ramifications that go beyond being fired from your job. Remember, too, that employers have the technology and the right to monitor your phone calls, voice mail, e-mail, and Internet activities.

16. **Behavior counts.** How you conduct yourself, how you interact with coworkers, and the way you approach your work all affect your success. Superiors considering you for a promotion usually take into account your work performance, how you deal with stress, how motivated you are, and how people like working with you.

17. **Act maturely.** Prove that you can work well without supervision and are dependable, responsible, and professional at all times.

18. **Keep your work space businesslike.** In most workplaces, it is acceptable for offices to reflect the personalities of their occupants as long as the overall decor is not offensive or unprofessional. A few personal touches are fine—photos, diplomas, awards, a few healthy plants. Racy posters and calendars or posted slogans that reflect a negative attitude, such as "I love my job; it's the work I hate" or "Is it Friday yet?" should be avoided, however.

19. **Be organized.** Set up a filing system that works for you. If an appropriate system is not obvious, ask a coworker for assistance, or get a book on developing organizational skills. The time you invest in getting organized will result in increased productivity. To avoid accumulating office clutter, you may want to set aside a few minutes at the beginning or end of each day to do housekeeping. Also, take time to set daily, weekly, and long-term priorities.

20. **Stay informed.** Unlike in school, where you were assigned reading material, on the job it's up to you to find and read material related to your position. You might consider reading industry trade journals and newsletters, competitors' sales literature, and a daily newspaper, among other resources.

Don't forget to include the Internet in your research. Check the Web regularly to see what's new and exciting in your field. Include in your searches sites of professional associations in your field, competitors of your company, companies in related fields, and vendors to your industry.

21. **Be receptive to new ideas.** Be willing to learn new skills and new ways of doing specific tasks. When possible, take the ball and run with it.

22. **Keep your personal life personal.** Relationship problems and financial difficulties should be dealt with outside the office. Involving coworkers in personal problems is unprofessional.

23. **Learn to accept criticism.** Try not to become defensive when criticized. Instead, learn from your mistakes.

24. **Know your strengths and weaknesses.** What do you enjoy? What gives you a sense of satisfaction? What types of tasks make you uncomfortable? Position yourself to take on those responsibilities for which you are best suited.

25. **Write down short-term (daily, weekly, and monthly) and long-term (one-year, five-year, and ten-year) goals.** Make the goals realistic and measurable. Evaluate yourself periodically. Revise your goals when necessary.

26. **Accept all responsibilities graciously.** Realize that in your first job, you may be asked to do entry-level tasks that do not fully utilize your education and skills. Complete those tasks with a good attitude, but seek opportunities to take on more challenging work.

27. **Accept the fact that you won't love every aspect of your job; few people do.** View each task as part of a bigger process aimed at accomplishing your goals. Also, first jobs are just that—first jobs. Rarely does someone stay in a first job for life. Gain all you can out of the experience.

28. **Remember that you won't be new forever.** Eventually, you'll get to know the ropes, just as your coworkers did. With a little enthusiasm, professionalism, and common sense, you'll be well on your way to success.

Tips for Working with Your Manager

Because there are likable people and unlikable people, it is natural that managers can fall into either category. If you're blessed with a good manager, you'll have the opportunity to learn from someone with experience and to develop a long-term professional relationship. If, on the other hand, you find that getting along with your manager is a challenge, swallow your pride and consider this an educational experience. Here are some tips for working with your manager:

1. **Understand your manager's position.** He most likely answers to another boss, who is interested only in performance and results. Be aware of your manager's position in the company and your position relative to others whom he manages.

2. **Communicate with your manager.** As in any relationship, good communication is important. Don't be afraid to tell your manager of your successes, failures, and goals. She can't help you if you don't make known what you want.

3. **Take the ball and run with it.** Most managers prefer that their staff assume some responsibility so that they don't need to micromanage. Find ways to help your manager get the job done.

4. **Accept criticism without becoming defensive.** Work on improving deficiencies and learn from your mistakes.

5. **Consider the situation as short term.** At some point in your career, you're likely to encounter a manager with whom your personality clashes. If you see no hope for developing a good working relationship with your manager, begin quietly looking for your next job. Continue to act professionally and responsibly, even if the situation gets rough. Don't treat this glitch in your career as a personal failure. Instead, see it for what it is, learn from the experience, and move on.

Managing Relationships on the Job

It would be a mistake to think that success in a job depends wholly on your level of expertise and performance. Good interpersonal skills can be just as important, if not more so. If your personal attributes and the culture of the hiring company don't merge, you may be in the wrong place. A situation of "bad chemistry" has serious ramifications. If you can't adjust to the corporate culture—or it to you—you could be out of a job again.

"Right chemistry" refers to the match of an employee's behavioral style and the required style of an employer and of a particular job—in addition to having the requisite skills. Interpersonal characteristics and cultural fit are highly important elements of professional success. Good social skills, a positive attitude, enthusiasm, and a sense of humor are vital. Here are some tips to help you establish successful relationships with your coworkers:

1. **Develop relationships in which you have mutual respect.** Mutual respect based on mutual gain is vital.

2. **Learn to manage the small-group relationship.** In school, for the most part you learned to work as an individual, but in companies, teamwork is the direction of the future.

3. **Make a point of getting involved with other people in the organization and their work.** Be friendly, but not to the point where talking takes time away from your work and impacts your productivity. It's good to have people on your side.

4. **Develop good interpersonal and communication skills.** Cultivate relationships with others through good verbal and written communication.

5. **Ask everyone questions.** Absorb information from all people you work with. Be respectful of other people's jobs.

6. **Pay attention to the actions and responses of others.** Listen and observe. What are people saying and doing? Involve others in your day-to-day decisions.

7. **Steer clear of office politics.** How effectively one deals with politics is just as important as how well one does the job. It can greatly influence whether you succeed or fail.

8. **Tips for becoming a team player:**

   a. **Develop a "team mentality."** Exhibit a good attitude.

   b. **Participate in group activities both during company time and after hours.** Group sports, such as softball and bowling, can provide great bonding experiences. Social gatherings can help make work settings more comfortable, but remember that your off-hours conduct should never be inappropriate or fodder for the gossip mill.

   c. **Show your team spirit; take pride in the team.** Support your coworkers. Contribute to team success. Share credit for accomplishments, and congratulate others on their successes.

9. **Traps to avoid:**

   a. **Forming cliques.** Participating in a clique makes a statement to people outside the group that they don't belong, possibly alienating people whom you may one day need on your side.

   b. **Sexual and racial comments.** Sexual harassment and bigoted language are not acceptable, even behind closed doors.

   c. **Passing judgment.** Avoid being critical of others. Your judgments could be wrong, and your comments will most likely get back to the person you criticized.

   d. **Kissing up to the boss.** You'll alienate coworkers and eventually management if you take this tack. It's appropriate to let your manager know how you're doing, but use appropriate forums, such as a monthly report.

   e. **Breaking a trust.** This is the quickest way to lose friends in the work environment.

   f. **Gossiping.** Talking about others is unprofessional. Talking about business issues outside work could be harmful to the business. Discretion is important. In business, gossip can get back to competitors, vendors, and suppliers. Be careful of what you say.

   g. **Socializing at work.** Have fun, but strike a balance between socializing and serious work. Also, balance your work life with your personal life. Having only coworkers as friends may be too limiting.

Finding a Mentor

Find a good mentor, and you'll greatly accelerate your on-the-job learning and increase your potential for success. A mentor should be someone you respect, admire, and like. Mentors can set good examples, teach procedures, help you see the big picture, solve problems, guide you toward your future, and provide perspective and emotional support. Women and minorities can especially benefit from mentoring, a system white males have used for years.

What's in the relationship for the mentor? Many professionals see mentoring as an opportunity to give back for their success. Some are flattered to have a new recruit admire them. Mentors also get the benefit of your loyalty and dedication. Your success may help ensure their success. They may look to you for help with special projects. You may also provide them with creativity and new perspectives in dealing with work situations.

To find a mentor, identify someone with solid experience and good interpersonal skills. Some companies have established mentoring programs through which you are paired with a willing coworker. Although it would be best to have a mentor within your own organization, you can also tap professional groups like SCORE (the Service Corps of Retired Executives) as sources of mentors. Be sensitive to your mentor's time constraints. Don't just take from the mentor, but also find ways you can help her do her job better. Realize that even mentors have a human side, and recognize their shortcomings while appreciating their positive attributes. Finally, when you eventually outgrow your mentor, don't forget who helped you get to that stage.

How You Will Be Evaluated

In school, you were accustomed to receiving midterm and final grades. In the real world, you'll most likely have performance reviews. The larger the company, the more formal the process tends to be. A performance review evaluates the quality of your work over a specific time period, usually a year.

In reviews, it is often the case that objective and subjective criteria are evaluated. For instance, a review might assess your achievement of short-term goals and progress made on long-term goals, as well as your attitude, ability to get along with others, and professionalism. Most likely, you will be rated with some form of grading system.

A performance review usually includes a salary review as well. Raises in most companies are not guaranteed, however. Poor individual performance, rough times for the company, or management changes can all influence a potential raise. Try to focus on your contribution to the company as the reason for a raise. Your "need" for more money is not really relevant in the company's eyes.

The most important part of a performance review should be a discussion of areas for improvement and the setting of new goals. Your task as an employee is to clarify any areas of your review you don't adequately understand, accept constructive criticism with grace, and express willingness to improve any problem areas.

The Importance of Staying Current

In today's fast-paced, competitive market, it is essential to stay current and informed—even when you have a job. By continuing to improve your skills and education, you not only improve your job performance (and hopefully your compensation), but you also greatly enhance your marketability should you need to resume a job hunt. Also, by keeping an active and curious mind you increase your job satisfaction and prevent burnout. Depending on your field, there are many avenues to self-improvement.

One of the most obvious ways to become more informed is through formal education. Take courses through your local college or your city's adult-education program. Many colleges now cater to working adults by offering courses in the evenings or on weekends. You do not have to complete a degree, but instead can dabble in a class or two to brush up on your writing, speaking, or computer skills. You will be surprised at how many others like you are taking classes and how understanding most professors are regarding the needs of working adult students. Returning to school can be a frightening experience for some, but most find the rewards well worth the initial apprehension.

In some cases, employers team up with local educators and corporate trainers to design appropriate courses or seminars to be offered in the workplace. This is something you may want to inquire about or suggest to your supervisor. Of course, if your employer already offers some additional training, you would be wise to jump at the opportunity.

Other opportunities for formal education include seminars and conferences sponsored by local professional organizations or trade associations. These seminars are often designed to meet a need common to people in your profession. They tend to be brief, focused, and highly informational—a good choice for those with little time. These classes offer another hidden but invaluable asset: the opportunity to network with other people in your field and learn through word of mouth about relevant news and technology. When attending such seminars, avoid the temptation to be a wallflower or to take a wait-and-see attitude. You may learn more by making small talk with the person next to you in the coffee line than you might have expected.

Networking groups represent a more formal way to reap the benefits of networking. These groups usually meet once a month and offer members the opportunity to exchange business cards, develop contacts, keep track of developments in their field, and get to know their competitors.

You can also join trade associations or professional organizations to keep on top of important developments in your field. Virtually every profession has a national association that offers a publication on developments in the field as well as updates on relevant legislation and technology. Even if you choose not to join your national or local professional or trade organization, it is still a good idea to check out these publications at your local library or on the Internet. When considering whether you should become involved, keep in mind that trade and professional organizations typically offer discounted student memberships and are often looking for leadership at the local or national level.

These same organizations also hold trade shows, where leaders in the field show off their latest products and rub elbows. You may find that after attending a few trade shows, you begin to recognize the names and faces of key industry players. They, in turn, may even get to know you!

Other opportunities for staying current might not initially come to mind. Some people choose to get an inside look at a particular type of business by doing temporary, freelance, or consulting work. Others choose to go straight to the source and ask for informational interviews with people in the industry (see page 37 for tips on how to conduct informational interviews).

Finally, it is important to keep an open and curious mind. Read newspapers and trade magazines to keep abreast of trends and issues that affect your field. Search the Internet on a regular basis for news about your field, related businesses, and your employer's competitors and vendors. Offer to cross-train at your place of employment or to assist your coworkers whenever you're able. By continuing the lifelong process of listening and learning, you will find that you become a sought-after and indispensable member of the work force.

Alternative Work Arrangements

Changing social values have resulted in employees demanding a more diverse array of work options to fit their lifestyles. A number of factors are contributing to this trend:

1. There is an increasing number of single-parent families.

2. More professional women and men want to raise their children while continuing their careers.

3. Older employees wish to postpone retirement but reduce their working hours.

4. Employees are more conscious of the amount of time they spend commuting.

5. Workers are placing more value on personal time.

6. More workers want to continue their education while employed.

You may find that one of these situations applies to you. Five types of work arrangements are most common:

Standard work schedule.   A forty-hour workweek is the most common arrangement. The forty-hour total usually does not include time for lunch. Typical business hours are from 8:30 A.M. or 9:00 A.M. to 5:00 P.M. or 5:30 P.M., Monday through Friday. Some businesses, however, may start at different hours. Construction companies, for instance, often start their day quite early, and restaurants may not open until 10:00 A.M.

Flextime.   A flextime schedule gives employees a choice of work hours. Some may prefer to start work early and finish early, whereas others may prefer to start work later and finish later. Employees are thus able to gear their schedules to optimum commuting times or child-care arrangements. Under this arrangement, all employees are required to be at work during certain hours of the day (called *core-time* hours); the flexible hours are on either end of the core time. Each employee must work a total of forty hours per week.

Job sharing.   In job sharing, two people divide the responsibilities of one regular full-time job. This type of arrangement is becoming more common, especially among women who wish to spend time at home with their children while continuing to work.

Compressed workweek.   By extending the workday beyond the standard eight hours, employees can create a schedule in which they work the required forty hours in a three- or four-day week.

Telecommuting.   With advances in technology, more people are able to avoid time-consuming commutes by operating out of their homes or satellite offices for some, if not all, of their workdays. Telecommuters keep in touch with coworkers by phone, fax, modem, and e-mail. In theory, using a laptop computer and a cell phone, employees can set up a virtual office anywhere.

When to Move On

Whether your first job is the best thing that ever happened to you or just so-so, there will probably come a time when you should consider exploring new opportunities. That time may come after a few months, several years, or longer. How do you know when you're ready? Take this short test:

1. I feel dissatisfied with my job.   ❑ yes   ❑ no

2. I argue frequently with my boss.   ❑ yes   ❑ no

3. I feel stifled in my position.   ❑ yes   ❑ no

4. I no longer feel challenged.   ❑ yes   ❑ no

5. I am not compensated fairly for my work.   ❑ yes   ❑ no

If you answered "yes" to any of these questions, you may want to think about moving on. Before taking action, consider the following variables:

1. Are there other opportunities in my field?   ❑ yes   ❑ no

2. Would I have to relocate to find a new job?   ❑ yes   ❑ no

3. Do I have enough experience to obtain a better position? ❑ yes   ❑ no

4. Does my current job have perks, such as health care
    benefits, flexible hours, or a convenient commute,
    that would be hard to replace?   ❑ yes   ❑ no

Exploring Your Options

Your job can easily turn into a security blanket. You are comfortable with your responsibilities and you know and like your coworkers. It's up to you to decide if those are good reasons to stay. Taking risks can be scary, but risks often result in the biggest gains.

Even if you're perfectly content in your current job, you should regularly read the local newspapers and relevant trade publications and also network in your field just in case you're forced by your employer to move on (let's face it—management turnover, reorganization, mergers, budget cuts, and layoffs mean no one is ever 100% secure) or you reach a point where you're ready for a change.

Regardless of your reason for moving on, try to explore your opportunities before leaving your current job. You can negotiate from a stronger position if you already have a job. Be discreet about your job search, and be professional if you do decide to leave. Do not burn any bridges. Give at least two weeks' notice to your employer, and try not to leave any projects unfinished. You'll want your employer to remember you favorably should you ever need a recommendation.

Should You Change Fields?

Beyond questioning whether your job is right for you, perhaps you're wondering whether you should change your career direction. You may have worked for several years in your field and felt unsatisfied. Or you may think other fields would offer more opportunities for growth. It's always a worthwhile endeavor to explore your options. And it's certainly not uncommon today to experience two or more careers during one's working life.

The bad news is that changing fields can be more difficult than finding a new job in the same field. Initially, you might have to take a pay cut and do entry-level work. The good news is that changing careers is exciting and very doable.

Before you leap into your next career, be sure to do the following:

1. **Examine your objectives.** Be sure that you are moving toward something, not just running away from your current work situation. Take a careful and objective look at whether you should seek a new job with a different company or a new career altogether.

2. **Read about your new field,** enough to know that your interests and talents are applicable. Check out the Internet, magazines, books, and newspapers.

3. **Speak to people currently working in your prospective field** to get their impressions about whether the work is satisfying and whether career opportunities seem to be growing or diminishing.

4. **Contact relevant associations and organizations** that can provide you with data and insights into the field.

5. **Be sure you have most of the skills relevant to your prospective field,** even if some of the terminology and procedures are unfamiliar to you. If you can find a niche that utilizes your existing skills, you'll likely start off at a higher level than you would otherwise. For example, a teacher who learns business skills could move into the field of corporate training.

6. **Begin to establish some contacts via networking** with people in the field. These people could become good sources for job leads.

7. **Check with your family** to see if they are supportive of your move.

8. **Talk with friends, teachers, and professional advisors** about your plans. Get their input on your intended move and whether they think it is a good decision for you. Although you don't have to take their advice, they may offer some ideas you hadn't considered.

9. **Examine the experiences and lifestyle** connected with this type of work. Do they suit your objectives and your personality?

You Can Do It!

Learning Objectives

In this chapter, you'll read case studies from people in many different careers who utilized a wide variety of techniques to ultimately find employment.

Every story is unique and is testimony to the fact that there's no single, direct path to career achievement, no easy answer to the question of how to get a job. From reading about their experiences, however, you'll gain a better understanding of all the steps you can take to increase your chances of job-hunting success.

Chapter 16

STRATEGIES in ACTION

Katelyn answered her phone, saying a silent prayer that it was the employer with whom she'd recently interviewed for a position as product manager. She had liked the company and found the employees she'd met to be extremely warm and energetic. It was a business clearly on the verge of major growth, with excellent prospects for its future. The product line that Katelyn would oversee was unique to the industry and had the potential to vault the company into a position of leadership.

In her most professional voice, she said, "Good morning. Katelyn speaking." Yes! It was the employer, and after a little friendly banter, he offered her the job. Before responding, Katelyn quickly thought back over all the work and effort that had gotten her to this moment—the many résumés she'd sent out, the cold calls she'd nervously made, the leads she'd followed, the networking, the numerous interviews, and finally, the negotiation process that had resulted in this wonderful offer. Katelyn took a deep breath and said, "When do I start?"

Success Stories

In this section, we present a sampling of quotations from some of the people we interviewed for *The Ultimate Job Hunter's Guidebook,* describing how they found their jobs. Their strategies vary from simply responding to a classified ad, to creatively transferring skills in one area to another, to aggressive networking combined with a stroke of good luck. When you read their stories, we hope you'll be inspired by their success and moved to action toward getting your own career off the ground.

> *I was attending classes during the day to become a paralegal and waitressing at night just to pay my bills. One of the regulars happened to be a partner in a prominent law firm. When I graduated, I gave him my résumé, and he gave me my first paralegal job.*
>
> Ilene, Paralegal

> *I sent a cover letter and my résumé to a major advertising agency in my area asking if they had any openings for a copywriter. They sent me a form rejection letter. I figured that was the end of it. But about two weeks later, I got a call from that agency's largest client, a major cruise line, seeking an in-house promotions writer. The agency had passed my résumé along. I had a brief interview with the manager, who hired me on the spot, saying the referral from the ad agency was all she needed to make her decision.*
>
> Jennifer, Promotions Writer

My roommate heard a radio station advertising for sales representatives. She called to request an interview. By the time the radio station returned her call several weeks later, she had accepted another position. I took her interview, with the radio station's permission, and got the job.

Jamie, Radio Sales Account Executive

I had answered an ad for a human resources representative for a major tourist attraction. I had three lengthy interviews over the course of a month. In the end, another candidate was selected. I was extremely disappointed because I had invested a lot of time and had been confident I would be chosen. Nonetheless, I sent notes to the people who'd interviewed me, thanking them for their consideration. I was glad I did, because a few weeks later the company called me back. They had another opening, and it was mine if I wanted it.

Ronnie, Human Resources Representative

I taught high-school math for several years, but my real passion was always physical fitness. I competed in two triathlons and many bodybuilding contests. I began counseling friends on how to lose weight and get in shape. They referred me to their friends, and eventually I was able to get a little side business going as a personal trainer. Once the business had a strong base, I decided to leave my teaching position, devoting all my time to a career as a fitness trainer. I love what I do and believe I've helped many people improve the quality of their lives by educating them on how to eat right and exercise for long-term health and fitness.

Russ, Fitness Trainer

For years, I was a nurse in a major hospital. I got to know many of the sales representatives from the pharmaceutical companies. I let one of the reps know I was looking to get out of nursing. I gave her a copy of my résumé, which she passed along to her sales manager, who eventually hired me.

Karen, Pharmaceutical Sales Representative

I studied marketing at college, but skiing is my real love. Fortunately, I was able to find a job that combined the two. I'm a marketing director for an upscale ski resort.

Gary, Marketing Director

I had little success answering classified ads with a traditional cover letter and résumé. I decided to try a unique approach. I created what essentially was a one-page flyer about me and used that with a targeted cover letter to apply for a job as a research technician. It helped me stand out from the other applicants, and I did end up getting interviews and eventually a job offer.

Paulina, Research Technician

I was flying home for the holidays, depressed that I still hadn't found a job. When I boarded the plane, I found someone already sitting in my seat. As it turned out, her last name was the same as mine, hence the seat mix-up. I ended up taking the seat next to her, and we chatted the entire flight. I told her I was seeking a management position for a manufacturing company. As luck would have it, she worked for a major manufacturer in my area and gave me the names of people to contact and also some inside information about the company's anticipated growth. Her tips were right on the money, and I had a job within a month.

Candy, Production Manager

I've always loved reading. I would have liked to become a children's author, but after several failed attempts, I faced the reality that I didn't have the literary talent necessary to be published. I wasn't ready to give up on my dream, however. I applied for and got a job as a sales representative for a major publisher of children's books. I truly believe in the quality of the books that we sell. And I get a great deal of personal satisfaction knowing that I am introducing literature to children through selling my company's books to schools, libraries, and bookstores.

Antonio, Sales Representative for book publisher

I did temporary work at a tourist bureau while I was job-hunting for a permanent marketing position. The tourist bureau had no full-time openings. However, the vice president to whom I reported soon left the company to start his own marketing consulting business. Because we had worked well together, he asked me to join him.

Paul, Marketing Consultant

To keep busy when I was searching for an IT job, I helped my dad set up a web page on the Internet for his company. He got so many compliments on it that some of his friends asked me to help design web pages for their businesses. Before I knew it, I was in business.

Daniel, Internet Designer

The human resources department of a health care company had me interview for the position of respiratory therapist. That interview lasted just a few minutes before the human resources representative decided I was qualified and sent me directly to the respiratory department manager, who would ultimately make the hiring decision. The manager was furious when I told him who I was and why I was there. He resented that human resources had not contacted him properly to schedule the interview. He was rude to me and spent the entire meeting fuming at the situation.

After the meeting I was upset, but decided to send the manager a gracious thank-you note anyway. Two days later he called to say he'd received my note. He apologized for his inappropriate behavior and offered me the job.

Jan, Respiratory Therapist

Like a lot of students in my graduating class, I got my degree and assumed I'd have no trouble finding a job. Wrong! I was a pilot and had dreams of flying Boeing 747s for one of the big airlines. Unfortunately, so did lots of other people, and it soon became apparent that I would be expected to "pay my dues" before I could join the elite rank of pilots who fly commercial jets.

I decided I wanted to live in Florida. So I took a stack of résumés, and starting at the northernmost point of the state, I began driving, stopping at every airport, big and small. I would look for a flight school at the airport, introduce myself to whoever was in charge and ask to leave a résumé behind. Eventually, I got lucky when I stopped at the airport in Sarasota. The manager said they were looking for a flight instructor and that my timing was perfect.

I was a flight instructor there for about a year before I got a job as a pilot for an overnight delivery service. A few years after that, I was finally able to get into a major airline as I'd dreamed and to fly commercial jets. It was a long haul, but I have to admit I learned a lot along the way.

Ravi, Commercial Pilot

I wanted to be a police officer from the time I could talk. When I was in high school, I worked at an amusement park during my summer vacation. One summer vacation from college, where I was majoring in law enforcement, I was moved into the security department at the amusement park and eventually promoted to head of security. My years at the park combined with my law enforcement degree helped me easily land my dream job as a police officer.

Todd, Police Officer

> "Go confidently in the direction of your dreams. Live the life you've imagined."
>
> *—Henry David Thoreau*

I was right out of school with a degree in advertising, but I had no contacts in the field. The first thing I did was to contact the local professional association for advertising executives, let them know I was job-hunting, and sent them a few copies of my résumé. Less than a week later, I received a call from an ad agency. Apparently, the agency had called the association requesting referrals for a production assistant.

Joan, Production Assistant

When my three children were young, it was always a challenge to find good domestic help. I was constantly searching for the perfect nanny, a decent housekeeper, or a likable mother's helper. After a while, I realized that many of my friends were asking me to use my experience and research to help them find domestic help. That's how I began my domestic employment agency, now in its eleventh year of business.

Rosie, Owner, domestic employment agency

I applied for an entry-level public relations job at a nonprofit organization that I had seen posted at my college. I was granted an interview, which involved a two-hour drive from my home. When I got to the interview, I learned that the person I was to meet had called in sick, and no one had thought to cancel my interview. One of her coworkers, feeling badly about the miscommunication, offered to interview me in her stead. We hit it off, and he recommended me for the job. I later learned that his recommendation was so strong that no one else was even interviewed.

Ayisha, Public Relations Coordinator

For 15 years, I was essentially a concert roadie, overseeing the lighting and pyrotechnic displays of various big-name rock groups as they performed around the world. When I hit my 30s, I realized I was tired of traveling and the frenetic pace of touring. I wanted a traditional job, one that would allow me to spend more time at home with my wife and two young children. Unfortunately, there weren't a lot of local businesses looking for pyro experts.

I knew I needed to step back and identify my strengths, the specific qualities that I could bring to another employer. A career test helped me realize that I had excellent organizational skills, worked well under intense deadlines, could juggle lots of details, got along well with coworkers, and was good at problem solving. Although it took many months to find just the right position, I eventually landed a job as a convention services manager in a major hotel. Pulling together all the details of a large convention required many of the skills I'd developed working on the road, ensuring concert performances ran smoothly. Now I'm home every night in time for dinner, I rarely travel out of town, and I get to spend much more time with my family.

Keith, Convention Services Manager

I was an aerobics instructor at several local gyms, but my dream was to eventually own my own fitness center where I could really help people to make healthy lifestyle changes. One of the gyms I was teaching at was on the verge of closing due to financial problems. The owners let it be known that they would be willing to sell for a song. I realized that this was the opportunity I'd been waiting for. With the help of friends, family, and a sizable bank loan, I was able to buy it.

I immediately revamped all the classes, hired new fitness instructors, brought in personal trainers, updated the exercise equipment, painted, renovated, and most importantly, focused on recruiting new members. Just one year later, the gym is no longer fledgling. It now operates in the black, membership has quadrupled, and it has become the leading gym in the area.

Cynthia, Owner, fitness center

I graduated with a degree in art but couldn't find a job in my field. Mostly to pay my rent but also as a creative outlet, I went to work in a local bakery as a cake decorator. Customers would often compliment me on my unique, artistic cake designs. One customer asked if I ever did any painting. When I told her my degree was in art, she hired me to paint a mural on her daughter's bedroom wall. She loved the work and began passing my name around to her many friends. I was hired to do everything from painting family portraits to designing custom Christmas cards. Eventually, I was able to get a couple of children's books I had written and illustrated published. While I still can't wholly support myself on my artwork, my business is continually growing, and I hope one day to work full-time as an artist.

Martin, Artist

I saw an ad in the paper seeking a creative marketing person for a software development company. I decided to try something a bit off-the-wall. I shipped my résumé in a big box along with a beach ball that had my name and phone number scrawled on it. In my cover letter I explained that I was the type of person who could "take the ball and run with it." My creative approach paid off—I got the interview and the job.

Avi, Vice President, Marketing

As an art history major, I had always dreamed of working in a museum. I frequented our local art museum and became friends with one of the researchers. When she mentioned she was leaving to take another position, I applied for her job. With her recommendation, I was hired.

Phillip, Museum Researcher

I went to school to become a paramedic. When I graduated, I was able to get a job with an ambulance company. There I learned about dealing with virtually every type of emergency and crisis. After several years, I decided to expand my horizons. I parlayed my hands-on experience as a paramedic into a career with an emergency management company that consulted with state and federal government in disaster planning.

Dayna, Emergency Management Consultant

I saw a job advertised for a reporter for a small weekly newspaper. Because I wanted the job so badly, I kept calling the publisher. I must have called four times a day for three weeks until he finally agreed to meet with me. Eventually, he hired me. He said someone as persistent as I had been had to be a good reporter.

Steven, Reporter

While I was a senior in college, I did volunteer work at the local chapter of the United Way. I got to know many of the staff people. When I graduated, they used their contacts to help me get a full-time position as an accountant with one of the agencies the United Way supports.

Mandy, Accountant

Success Story

Can you guess who? . . .

Failed in business	age 22
Ran for legislature and was defeated	age 23
Again failed in business	age 24
Elected to legislature	age 25
Sweetheart died	age 26
Had a nervous breakdown	age 27
Defeated for speaker	age 29
Defeated for Congress	age 34
Elected to Congress	age 37
Defeated for Congress	age 39
Defeated for Senate	age 46
Defeated for vice president	age 47
Defeated for Senate	age 49
Elected president of the United States	age 51

That man was Abraham Lincoln.

Permission to reprint granted by Ann Landers and Creators Syndicate.

I had been seeking a position as an administrative assistant for several months. To help pay the bills but keep my days open for interviews, I worked nights cleaning offices. One of the offices I cleaned belonged to a law firm, and I became friendly with a couple of the lawyers who worked late. They helped me get an interview at their firm when a position became available. Now someone cleans my office.

Leah, Administrative Assistant

I was seeking an entry-level position with an engineering firm. The owner of one of the companies I applied to was an alumnus of my college and agreed to interview me for that reason. As it turns out, we hit it off, and he hired me.

Ross, Engineer

I volunteered as a reporter for my college newspaper. One of the stories I wrote was about credit card fraud, and I interviewed several bankers in my area for information. I made sure they each received a copy of the article when it was published, along with a thank-you note for their time. Two months later when I graduated, I contacted these bankers again to let them know I was seeking a job in the banking industry. One of them had an opening in his bank's credit card division and referred me for the job.

Sharon, Credit Analyst

For years I stayed home taking care of my four young children. When the youngest started school, I felt lost. I wanted to work but didn't know what kind of job I could do. It had been years since I had held a paying job. Fortunately, I was able to convince an employer that my qualities as a mother—detail oriented, highly organized, creative, and extremely patient—were transferable to the type of position she needed to fill.

Linda, Nursing Home Manager

I wrote a term paper my senior year about child abuse. As part of my research, I interviewed several social workers. When I graduated, one of them helped me get a wonderful job in a child psychologist's office.

Thomas, Behavioral Therapist

When I was growing up, my family was very interested in the stock market. I learned a great deal about investing. I went to college for accounting and found that my knowledge of the financial markets came in handy. I had no problem combining the two into a career.

Dawn, Financial Planner

I was looking for a computer programming position. While job searching, I managed to obtain a couple of freelance programming jobs, which then led to additional work. Before I knew it, I was working full-time as an independent programmer. I hadn't even considered self-employment. Now I don't think I would ever consider working for someone else.

Sherry, Computer Programmer

I had worked as a secretary for about five years. I knew I was ready for a new challenge but didn't know what direction to go in. Then I became pregnant. At one of my obstetrical visits, I was given an ultrasound test, which allowed me to see the fetus moving around in my belly. I found it fascinating. After I had the baby, I began attending night school to become an ultrasound technician. Now I get to share the joy of others seeing their babies for the first time.

Lisa, Ultrasound Technician

During my college summer vacations, I volunteered at a local animal shelter. In addition to some great experience, I got to know all the local veterinarians. When I graduated, a veterinarian who remembered me from the shelter offered me a job.

Ken, Veterinary Assistant

I interviewed with an editor of a small weekly newspaper to be a freelance writer. While we chatted, he mentioned that the publisher was planning to start a new magazine targeted at women. He introduced me to the publisher, and within a week I was hired full-time as editor.

Maureen, Magazine Editor

I was always very overweight. In college, I decided to do something about it. I began going to a nutritionist for counseling. I became so interested in the field, I changed my major from nursing to nutrition and eventually went to work at the practice where I first learned how to manage my own weight problem.

Patti, Nutritionist

I had applied for numerous teaching jobs using conventional methods and had been unsuccessful. One day, in a fit of desperation, I walked into a local college, located the chairperson for the English department, and hastily explained why I would be an excellent candidate for her next open position. She agreed, and as luck would have it, she had an opening. I walked out with a job offer in less than thirty minutes.

Melissa, English Professor

In high school, I worked in a motorcycle parts store nights and weekends. My boss really liked me and told me that there would always be a place for me in his company. I went to college and majored in management. When I graduated, I called my old boss, hoping he would still remember me. By then his business had grown to four stores. He did remember me and lived up to his word. He hired me to manage his entire operation.

James, Operations Manager

I interviewed for a position as a buyer for a major retailer. In the course of our conversation, the interviewer happened to mention that he loved jelly beans. The next day, I sent him a bag of gourmet jelly beans along with a thank-you note, mentioning how I'd been able to find this unique product for a great price, and I looked forward to applying those same skills in my next job. I got the position, and to this day keep a jar of jelly beans on my desk.

Robin, Retail Buyer

> "Nothing good was ever achieved without enthusiasm."
>
> —*Ralph Waldo Emerson*

I began as an administrative assistant for a property management company. Initially, my work involved mostly clerical tasks, but as the business grew and we acquired more clients, I took on more property management responsibilities. I began taking night courses in real estate management. Soon after that I was promoted to property manager and had to hire my own administrative assistant.

Chen, Property Manager

I studied to become a teacher, but when I graduated, no jobs were available at local schools. Reading the classified ads one day, I saw several positions advertised for corporate training associates. I found I had most of the required skills and decided to apply. Now I work for a large computer company "teaching" new hires our policies and procedures.

Stephen, Corporate Training Associate

I studied dance performance all through college. After graduation, I went to numerous auditions and soon learned that there were many more dancers than there were positions available. Eventually, I was able to get a job that kept me involved in the dance profession and also helped me develop management expertise. I became a performance coordinator for a traveling dance company.

Carol, Dance Performance Coordinator

I was a customer service representative for the local telephone company. With increased automation, the company was experiencing numerous layoffs. It soon became apparent that my position would be eliminated. I contacted the local electric company and was hired because of my experience working for a utility company.

Tom, Customer Service Representative

I was working as a nurse for a pediatrician. One day another nurse came into the office and asked the pediatrician I worked for to precept, or mentor, her through her nurse practitioner program. The doctor replied, "If I were going to precept anyone, it would be Marilyn." I looked up in disbelief. I had never considered going on for an advanced degree and had no idea that my employer would be so supportive. I seized the opportunity, took him up on his offer, and am now very satisfied with my job as a nurse practitioner.

Marilyn, Nurse Practitioner

I placed a positions-wanted ad in an advertising trade journal for an electronic art specialist. I got calls from a few ad agencies, a couple of companies with in-house graphics departments, and a statewide newspaper. I chose the newspaper because it seemed to present the most opportunity for long-term growth.

David, Electronic Art Specialist

We moved around a lot for my husband's job, and I became quite skilled at buying and selling houses. I eventually got my real estate license and became a real estate salesperson.

Irene, Realtor

After college graduation, I interned in the news department at a local TV station. I was envious of my friends who were making big money while I was essentially a volunteer, but I knew my time would come. I spent most days in the sports department. Because it was understaffed, I was frequently given reporting assignments that might otherwise have gone to more seasoned reporters. Eventually, the sports department was given the budget to

The Victor

C. W. Longenecker

If you think you are beaten, you are.
If you think you dare not, you don't.
If you like to win but think you can't,
It's almost a cinch you won't.
If you think you'll lose, you're lost.
For out in the world we find
Success begins with a fellow's will.
It's all in the state of mind.
If you think you are outclassed, you are.
You've got to think high to rise.
You've got to be sure of yourself before
You can ever win the prize.
Life's battles don't always go
To the stronger or faster man.
But sooner or later, the man who wins
Is the man who thinks he can.

expand. I was hired full-time as a sports reporter and am currently working toward becoming a sports anchor.

Dan, Sports Reporter

I studied liberal arts in college and wasn't quite sure exactly what career I was going to pursue. I joined a club of women entrepreneurs for the purposes of networking and learning what types of careers other women had. I became friends with a woman who owned a vocational school. One day she mentioned that she was in a jam because her communications skills teacher had just quit and classes were scheduled to start in three days. Since I was unemployed and felt I had good communications skills, I offered to substitute until she could find a replacement. The first class went so well, she offered me the job full-time.

Diane, Teacher

I studied cosmetology in my home country, Germany. After I immigrated to the United States, I learned that a company that manufactured a line of cosmetics I liked was planning to expand into this country. I contacted them, explained my familiarity with their products and knowledge of the American market, and was hired as a marketing consultant. Eventually, I was promoted to vice president of the North American division of the company.

Inge, Vice President, cosmetics company

Failures Who Became Successes

Gain inspiration and motivation from these "failures":

- Albert Einstein was 4 years old before he could speak.
- Isaac Newton did poorly in grade school and was considered "unpromising."
- Beethoven's music teacher once said of him, "As a composer, he is hopeless."
- When Thomas Edison was a youngster, his teacher told him he was too stupid to learn anything. He was counseled to go into a field where he might succeed by virtue of his pleasant personality.
- F. W. Woolworth got a job in a dry goods store when he was 21, but his employer would not permit him to wait on customers because he "didn't have enough sense to close a sale."
- Michael Jordan was cut from his high school basketball team.
- Boston Celtics Hall of Famer Bob Cousy suffered the same fate.
- A newspaper editor fired Walt Disney because he "lacked imagination and had no good ideas."
- Winston Churchill failed the sixth grade and had to repeat it because he did not complete the tests that were required for promotion.
- Babe Ruth struck out 1,300 times—a major league record.

I am a stay-at-home mom. One day when my kids were napping, I painted a floral design on a watering can I had in my garage. My mother-in-law happened to see it when visiting and asked if I could make some more for her upcoming garden club crafts fair. I painted seventeen watering cans, and they all sold. Then I began painting on all kinds of objects, from glass vases to ceramic planters. I now sell my works to about a dozen retail establishments in my area. The painting gives me a creative outlet and an income while allowing me to be a stay-at-home mom.

Sophie, Artist

I was about to graduate with a degree in architectural engineering technology when I came to the realization that I didn't enjoy the field and was not looking forward to my career. Fortunately, I had a couple of professors who liked me and recognized my work ethic. Using their contacts, they helped me get a job in computer software development for a major defense contractor. My new career choice is much better suited to my personality and interests. Best of all, my employer is paying for me to continue my education in the computer field.

Ray, Software Developer

I had been at home for years. I'd always followed my husband's career and needed to be available to entertain important business guests, organize my husband's travels, and research the never-ending array of new hometowns. Eventually, I decided I needed a career of my own. I was terrified and felt low on self-confidence and experience. With the help of a career counselor, I developed a wonderful functional résumé that stressed my organizational and hospitality skills as well as my experience with international guests. I now work for a major hotel as an events planner and utilize my life's experience and skills.

Sylvie, Events Planner

I'd always worked summer jobs at our local beach. When I was in high school, a seasonal position at the ice cream stand or hotel front desk seemed convenient, if not especially educational. During rainy days, I really minded the slow times and hated waiting around for a customer to come in. Something interesting happened, though. Since I often worked alone in the evenings, the patrol officers on beat would usually check in on me to make sure everything was okay. Anxious for conversation, I began to pass the time by asking them about their day and the job. Soon, I had a new group of friends and some real insights into the daily duties of a police officer. I decided to use that summer's income to get a degree in criminal justice. Now I'm the one checking in on the summer help.

Michelle, Police Officer

My little girl was born prematurely, necessitating a long stay in the hospital. I spent hours rocking her in the hospital nursery. I came to know the nurses on the floor. I listened to them talk with each other. I watched what duties they had on their shifts and asked them a lot of questions. After my daughter was well, we occasionally returned to the hospital for a visit. The nurses on duty encouraged me to investigate careers in nursing. When my child started preschool, I took a position as a nurse's aide. I learned of scholarships available to those planning to enter a career in nursing. Today, I proudly wear the title of registered nurse after my name.

Tracy, Registered Nurse

I took a work-study job with the buildings and grounds department at the college I attended. I loved the work because I got a chance to solve all sorts of maintenance problems at the school. The CAD department needed a lot

"Whatever you can do or dream you can, begin it. Boldness has power, genius, and magic in it. Begin it now."

—*Goethe*

of help planning and installing some new cabinetry in their new office space, and I came to know everyone there really well. I got my degree in architectural design and my first job as CAD manager for the campus.

Chris, Architect

EXERCISE   Answer the following questions.

1. Having read through these success stories, what themes emerge? What can you learn from the experiences of these individuals?

2. Think of your own friends and family members. Are their careers in line with the subject they majored in at school? Have they held the same job for many years or moved on? How have their careers progressed?

3. Write down the names of at least three people you know who hold jobs you think are interesting. Within the next few days, contact those people and ask them how they obtained their jobs. What can you learn from their career experiences?

1. _____

2. _____

3. _____

Advice from Those Who've Made It

Many of the people we spoke with while writing *The Ultimate Job Hunter's Guidebook* were willing to share advice about job hunting and career success. Here, briefly, are some of the thoughts that emerged from those conversations.

1. To succeed, choose a career you love.

2. Keep your eyes open for any and every opportunity. Then go for it!

3. Make your own breaks.

4. Learn something from every task and every job. It all comes in handy someday in some way you often can't foresee at the time.

5. Nobody is indispensable, especially you.

6. Learn from all the people you meet. Everyone has some special quality, skill, or talent.

7. Every problem is an opportunity in disguise.

8. Don't sweat the small stuff, and remember, most stuff is small.

9. Seek out challenges. Your greatest personal satisfaction will come from difficult achievements.

10. Take setbacks in stride. Learn from your failures, and move on.

11. Don't make the same mistake twice.

12. Cultivate your talents. Work on improving your deficiencies.

13. Practice your skills. Even the best artists, performers, athletes, and so on practice.

14. Persistence will get you almost anything eventually.

15. Try to make the right decisions in life. Rectify wrong decisions as hastily as possible.

16. Don't get caught up in the day-to-day stresses. Focus on the positive aspects of the big picture.

17. Work toward long-term goals, but enjoy life today.

18. Take responsibility for your actions, good or bad.

19. Don't spend time worrying about past mistakes. Live in the present.

20. Become the most positive, enthusiastic person you know.

21. Be decisive, even if it means you are sometimes wrong.

22. Find a comfortable balance between work and family.

23. Commit yourself to becoming a lifelong learner.

24. Character counts.

25. Be a nice person.

As you embark on your career, you'll be creating your own success stories and developing your own ideas about how to advance in the workplace. Write to us about your experiences. We'd love to hear about them and possibly even include them in the next edition of *The Ultimate Job Hunter's Guidebook*. Be sure to include your name, address, phone number, and e-mail address, so we can contact you.

Send submissions to:

Houghton Mifflin Company
College Business
222 Berkeley Street
Boston, MA 02116
college_bus@hmco.com

INDEX